D1751584

CHANGING MINDS:
A Journey of Awakening
— Recognition —

by Dr. Frank E. Allen and
Dr. Kathleen Allen-Weber

Copyright © 2019 Frank E. Allen, Ed.D. and
Kathleen Allen-Weber, Ph.D.

All rights reserved. Except for use in a review, the reproduction or utilization of this work in whole or in part in any form by any electronic, mechanical, or other means, including photocopy, recording, or in any information storage or retrieval system, is forbidden without the written permission from the authors, Frank Allen and Kathleen Allen-Weber.

Library of Congress Cataloging-in-Publication Data

Names: Allen, Frank E., Allen-Weber, Kathleen, authors
Title: Changing Minds The Invitation: Recognition
Series: Changing Minds
ISBN: 978-1-0906-2266-2
Subjects: Personal Growth / Consciousness / Mindfulness

Printed in the United States of America

"Be patient toward all that is unsolved in your heart and try to love the questions themselves, like locked rooms and like books that are now written in a foreign tongue. Do not now seek the answers, which cannot be given you because you would not be able to live them. And the point is, to live everything. Live the questions now. Perhaps you will then gradually, without noticing it, live along some distant day into the answer."

Rainer Maria Rilke

Acknowledgements

If we were to be completely honest and remain consistent with what we present in these books, everyone we have ever interacted with would need to be acknowledged. Their particular influence in our lives may vary, but all of them are part of our *Journey*. So we thank them.

There are those, however, whose influence in our lives has been greater. This would include family, friends, colleagues, our clients, and all those who have participated in our workshops. We acknowledge all of these for their trust, support, and encouragement.

There are also those who have impacted us in even deeper ways. These are our mentors, our spiritual teachers, and the authors who have inspired us. We would not be where we are without them. We give thanks to them all.

We hold a particularly deep debt of gratitude to our spouses—Cindy Myska and Alan Weber. They are the ones who have loved us through this entire endeavor. And they have made room for all the time and attention we have needed to develop, write-and rewrite—this trilogy.

Finally, there is no way we could ever thank Alan Weber enough for his contribution in helping edit and get this book out. This work would not be what it is without his keen eye, his excellent wordsmithing, and his "above and beyond" attention to the details of the formatting.

Table of Contents

Acknowledgements

Notes to the Reader

The Invitation

The Priceless Treasure   1

1   The Title: *Changing Minds*   8

2   The Paradoxical Journey   16

3   Recognition   22

4   The Bear and the Reindeer   27

5   The Reindeer with a "Halo"   32

6   Parallel Universes   35

7   Characteristics of the Parallel Universes   40

8   The Impeccability of Each Universe   46

9   Dreaming and the Dreamer   53

10   Not One Self, but Two   60

11   The Witness and the Observer   65

12   Waking from the Dream   69

13	Form and Content	74
14	Form and Content: Purpose	79
15	Form and Content: Practice	83
16	Not "It" but Not "Not It"	87
17	Cause and Effect	92
18	Source of Judgment	98
19	Honor but Not Condone	103
20	Time as Sleight of Hand	108
21	You Chose In, You Choose Out	114
22	Awakening: What It Is	118
23	Awakening: How It Works	123
24	Where to from Here?	127
	Glossary of Terms	135
	Quotes and Author Information	141

Notes to the Reader

We consider this trilogy of books our contribution to *Consciousness*. We know that we are merely contributors because of those who have preceded us in its exploration, and for those we know will follow to make their contributions as well. In that sense, we are all simply learning, growing, evolving, and moving forward to *Awakening*.

The *Journey of Awakening* is neither simple nor easy. Taking the *Journey* challenges everything we have been taught, and thus everything we believe. This book, whose theme is **Recognition**, is the first of the trilogy, and takes an initial look at how we do our lives, and the results of those choices so we can begin to *Awaken*. We hold *Awakening* as the end goal of a *Journey* through our *Minds*. That *Journey* takes place as we deepen our appreciation of the *Mind*, that is, the part that contains all our thoughts—useful or useless—and all our experiences—positive and negative.

We all intuitively know there is something that transcends our human condition, our human conditioning. These three books lay out a vision of what that is, what blocks our awareness of it, and what we need to do to *Awaken*. As such, *Awakening* would be synonymous with full remembrance of *Who We Are* in *Truth*.

We honor and respect our lives as we currently experience them on this plane of existence (as bodies in this world), for that is where we must begin our *Journey*. But we also know that this is not where *Awakening* takes place. We are profoundly grateful for that part in each of us that will not settle for the ephemeral offerings of this world, the part that knows better, that has never fully forgotten *Truth*. We invite you, the Reader, to join us as together, we reach for something much greater in our travels on this *Journey of Awakening*.

As for the specific details of the writing, we wish to point out that we have capitalized and italicized certain key words, like *Journey, Awakening, Love,* and *Reality*, throughout the trilogy as pointers towards the *Truth* we seek to remember. The capitalizations are reminders that these transcendent ideas are not of our making, and are not found on the plane of existence where we usually live. Such ideas cannot really be taught or learned, they can only be remembered. That remembering is the focus of these books. We provide a "Glossary of Terms" at the back of the book that explains new terms and differentiates between potentially confusing pairs of words, such as *Mind*/mind and *Truth*/truth.

We have written these books being as mindful as we can of all the ways in which you will intersect them. In addition to capitalizing and italicizing key words as pointers, we have also bolded the theme of this book, **Recognition**, whenever it appears in order to emphasize our objective. We also bold and italicize the title of each chapter the first time it appears and the title of the trilogy, ***Changing Minds***, throughout all three books. To better connect with you, the Reader, and to be gender sensitive, we have used "he" and "she" in alternating chapters.

We have done all these things to eliminate as many distractions as possible, and to help you always keep the goal in mind: *Awakening*.

We understand that what we present and the way we present it may not resonate with everyone. But if it speaks to you, we strongly encourage you to "try it on." Challenge your beliefs. See if your life is different—at least, how differently you feel about your life!

We deeply appreciate your being a part of our *Journey* and wish you Godspeed as you progress.

The Invitation

We begin our inquiry into the *Journey of Awakening* by addressing the core construct upon which our theory and this trilogy rests: **Changing Minds**. We must first make a critical distinction—that between **Changing Minds** and *changing your mind about* something. We cannot overemphasize how radically different these two concepts are. For a quick introduction into these two, we invite you to look at the "Glossary of Terms" found at the end of this book.

Changing Minds is altogether different from the act of merely *changing your mind about* something. When you *change your mind about* something, you simply alter ideas that already exist in your mind. You might gain new information that changes your previous opinion about something. Or, it may simply be that as you grow older, your thinking matures and you understand things in a way that was not possible for you before.

Changing Minds, on the other hand, reflects a shift to an entirely different realm of *Consciousness*, where thought itself is processed differently. It is in no way a simple modification of some pre-existing idea. It does not look backward to what you thought before, nor does it involve your personal judgment or evaluation. When you *Change Minds*, you move from a mind that has prejudices and preconceived notions to a *Mind* that is not imprisoned in all your acquired judgments. It is a Mind that is completely open to *Truth*. When you *Change Minds*, the focus shifts from self-preservation to relationship, relationship with your *Self*, your world, and your relationship with everything and everyone in it.

Most often, we do not understand or appreciate that the context of our life experience is relationship. In fact, we are usually not even aware that relationship is all there is, that the very essence of "I" (who I think I am) is defined in relationship to everything that "I" is not. The entirety of my experience of "me" is found in my relationship to everything and everyone in "my" world. *Consciousness* can be thought of as the interface between what I think of as "me" inside my skin, and what I think of as "not me" outside that skin: "my" world. And that is unique and private for each one of us. "My" world is different from "your" world, because "I" am not "you." Exploring these ideas about relationship becomes the process through which we evolve, and through which *Awakening* takes place.

Such a *Journey of Awakening* is critical because we humans are, for the most part, unconscious. We are asleep. We do not know or understand what is actually taking place in our experience of living in this world. We are prisoners of conditioned, pre-programmed ways of thinking that retard the evolution or awareness of *Consciousness*. But what happens when we break away from that thinking and dare to question our basic assumptions about life?

If human experience is not what it seems to be, it becomes critical to discover just what it is, so we can make better choices and be in a better position to accept responsibility for those choices. And we must remember that *Life is Process.* This increases both our patience and our willingness to slow down, to choose, and to grasp the opportunity that **Changing Minds** presents. When we understand what is really going on, we are less caught up in the specific events of our lives. We are less focused on the particulars of *what* is happening, of *who* is doing *what* to *whom,* and are able to go back and challenge the very root of what we think we see, feel, experience—what we think we know.

This trilogy elaborates a path towards *Awakening.* The theme of Book I is **Recognition.** Therein, we establish a theoretical framework that defines and clarifies what the *Journey of Awakening* is about. We look closely at how we live our lives and the consistently disappointing results we obtain by doing things the way we now do. **Recognition** is not only about identifying what we do *not* want, it is also about finding a new direction, discovering what we *do* want.

The theme of Book II is **Relinquishment.** In it, we look at all the obstacles we encounter along the way as we move toward greater *Consciousness.* If we do not specifically identify and target those obstacles, how is it possible to overcome them and advance on our *Journey?* Ironically, **Relinquishment** is not about giving up something of real value. Rather, it is willingly letting go of everything that stands in the way of what is genuinely valuable, all that we truly want.

Finally, the theme of Book III is **Restoration.** In this third volume, we take a close look at all the components of the *Practice* we must develop in order to advance on this *Journey of Awakening.* It is indeed a *Practice,* because we have years and years of habits and conditioned thinking to change—perhaps to overcome and entirely replace. This can occur only through a committed and disciplined *Practice* that acknowledges and makes space for our humanity, while helping us move forward and keep our focus on the ultimate goal: *Awakening*.

On some level, we all know that *Truth* is true. What is not true is not true and can never be true. So what stands in the way of our acknowledging and living from this? Many things slow us down: general anesthesia of the mind, fear of exposure and punishment for what we have replaced *Truth* with in our lives. What then ensues is the constant need for judgment to protect what we perceive as our fragile "self." And of course, there is always that part of us that we must concede does not want to know the *Truth*.

How do we learn to *see* differently? How do we unlearn everything we have learned in our lifetimes? We do so by becoming more conscious of what we believe, then challenging and surrendering those beliefs that are not true. We begin to take responsibility not for *what* happens in our lives, but for our *experience* of what happens. We come to understand that we alone give our world all the meaning it has for us, and that whatever we are experiencing is of our own making. It is a challenge, but it is also an invitation. It is, in fact, our invitation to you.

Let the journey begin...

The Priceless Treasure

This is a book about *Awakening* to a higher *Consciousness*, through a *Process* we call **Changing Minds**. We begin with a story about a man seeking a priceless treasure.

> There once was a very poor man who had a dream one night in which it was revealed to him that the next day, he would come upon a priceless treasure that would change his life forever. This treasure beyond all value would be his alone.
>
> The poor man awoke, amazed and expectant. He was walking to work along a dirt road when all of a sudden, he chanced upon a turbaned man sitting under a tree. The man was sitting alone, serenely contemplating a huge, perfectly shaped pearl in his hand.

The poor man gasped as he realized that this must be the priceless treasure foretold him! He approached the turbaned man and said: "Give me the pearl, for this night, I had a dream that foretold that a priceless treasure would be mine."

The turbaned man looked at the poor man and without a word, smiled and handed the poor man the pearl.

The poor man began his journey home, dreaming already of how his life would change. He would never again have to think about where the next meal was coming from. He imagined how he would surprise his family and friends, and how he would finally have his revenge on all those who had rejected him. He would sell the pearl, buy new clothes, a new home and new furnishings. He would dazzle those who had despised him. Now instead of heaping scorn on him, they would come to him begging for his help. How dramatically his life would change!

Suddenly, the poor man carrying the pearl stopped dead in his tracks. He cocked his head to one side, aware of the growing sadness he felt. He was startled to realize that *none* of these things would change anything at all for him. None of these things would make him truly happy.

He turned around and raced back to find the turbaned man sitting serenely in the same place under the same tree.

Breathless from running, the poor man stood a moment before the turbaned man, unable to speak a word. He held the pearl out as he looked deep into the eyes of the turbaned man. "Please take back this pearl...," he implored.

Then with a shy smile, he completed his request: "...and give me the priceless treasure. Tell me how you gave the pearl away."

This is a book that can teach you how to "give the pearl away." It is an exquisite metaphor for the overarching theme of this trilogy we have named ***Changing Minds***. At the onset of the story, the poor man was clinging to ideas and things and even fantasies he thought could make him happy: possessions, revenge, exalted status. But as the story ends, it becomes clear the poor man did not just *change his mind about* the pearl and how it would affect his life. Instead, he stopped "dead in his tracks" because he suddenly saw through his illusions to the *Truth* that none of those things would make him happy.

A new *Consciousness* arose within him, challenging all his previous ideas, and opening his mind to the possibility that the "treasure" was something other than the pearl. He C*hanged Minds*, from the mind guided by his ego that promised a delusional version of self-satisfaction, to the mind guided by *Spirit that* promised only *Truth*. But he had to be willing to set aside all he thought he knew in order to "see" differently, and when he did, he rushed back to request the treasure he truly sought.

This book is about *Consciousness*. It is about the choice each one of us faces each moment between everything we think we know (with all that thinking promises), and the *Truth* available to be known (with all that *Truth* promises to reveal). There are aspects of our approach to *Consciousness* that are not novel. Some of the ideas presented here have been taught and written about for centuries. In 1676, Isaac Newton, English physicist, mathematician, astronomer, alchemist, inventor, theologian and natural philosopher, wrote these words in a letter to a rival: "If I have seen further than others, it is by standing upon the shoulders of giants."

In a similar way, our far-seeing predecessors have elevated us, making it possible to look farther and understand better the workings of the *Mind*. We acknowledge those "giants" as we move deeper into a *Process* we call *Awakening*. What is *Awakening*? As *Consciousness* evolves, it transcends the limits and the suffering inherent in the human condition. Like the poor man in the analogy above, we no longer see things as we did before, and our lives are completely transformed. The three books of this trilogy lay out a vision of just what this evolution of *Consciousness* entails, what blocks our awareness of it, and what we can do to advance our goal of *Awakening*.

Our work adds a unique lens and a new vocabulary that represents the distillation and integration of what we have been studying and applying in our own lives over the past 35 years. It more clearly explains the vital role our conscious and unconscious thinking plays in our behavior. It all begins with the initial choice we make between ego and *Spirit*, illusion and *Truth*. Like the poor man seeking the treasure, we can look with our eyes for the pearl, or we can open our minds to a different possibility that offers far more than the pearl could ever bring.

The purpose of this trilogy is to provide a coherent description of the power of belief, which dictates how we live our lives. Aligned with ego, our lives are grossly distorted and limited. Aligned with *Spirit*, our possibilities are limitless. But beyond the examination of what we think and believe, theory is most useful when we know how to apply it— when it fundamentally changes our lives. That is our end goal.

Why this work now? It has always been true that before a certain level of *Consciousness* is attained, the "collective we" cannot really *do* or change anything. It is critical to note, however, that *Truth* is never changed simply because there are those who do not understand it, or are not ready to accept it. Think of the Europeans who fervently believed the world was flat and who feared to sail beyond the visible horizon—until Christopher Columbus first did. Or those in the sports world who did not think it possible to run the mile in less than four minutes—until Roger Bannister first did. Once that level of *Consciousness* is raised, as it was with Columbus in 1492 and with Bannister in 1954, everything changes. How much has our *Consciousness* changed since then? What else is possible?

We acknowledge the radical edge of such an undertaking and are fully aware that **Changing Minds** has the potential to redefine what we think we know about ourselves, our worlds, and how we experience our lives. On a personal level, it is inevitable that each of us will encounter our greatest resistances, where the deepest aspects of ourselves are hidden. But this is where true freedom lies. We may even come to see that we have spent our lives looking at life through a keyhole—and then realize how much more there is to see, to *know*.

This new understanding is tantamount to a slow-motion, complete reformatting of our mental hard drives. It will break up our notions of reality and question the validity of what we believe. The process is relentless, its scope is all-encompassing, its coverage complete. It has *no* exceptions. So why do it? Because we are finally ready to remember that *Truth* is true. And despite our hesitation, in truth, we want nothing less.

Victor Hugo, the great 19th-century French poet and novelist, is credited with having said, "There is nothing more powerful than an idea whose time has come." We interpret that to mean that a single novel distinction has transformational power that only occurs when "the time is right." This points towards the power of the idea itself, but it also implies a readiness for the idea to be accepted. Throughout history, brilliant, even profound ideas have sometimes fallen on deaf ears because the time for the idea had not yet come. The listeners, for whatever reason, were unable—or perhaps not ready—to hear.

We must respect that there are inherent limits in the progressive development of *Consciousness*. There is no way around the fact that a six-year-old child cannot comprehend what a teenager can, and a young adolescent cannot understand what a mature adult is able to. Each of us is only able to hear what we can in each moment in time, and then, only if we are ready to hear it.

This trilogy proposes that **Changing Minds** is the "idea whose time has come." Human consciousness has now reached a pivotal junction which enables us to "hear" and make a critical advancement. The heart of this *Process* is understanding the "self" and how it operates. The time for doing so is *now*.

The fact that you are reading this book signals some degree of readiness on your part. Ready for what, you may ask? We would suggest that you are ready to learn, ready to be surprised, ready to engage in life differently. You are ready to challenge what you think you know, perhaps even who you think you are. Like the poor man with his perfect pearl stopped "dead in his tracks," you are ready to see through all those things you thought would make you happy and discover the real "treasure" available to you. You are ready to take a step forward on your own *Journey of Awakening*.

1

The Title: *Changing Minds*

"There is no passion to be found in playing small—in settling for a life that is less than the one you are capable of living." Nelson Mandela

Changing Minds is at the heart of the process of *Awakening*. We highlight the contrast between *Changing Minds* and *changing your mind about* something with the use of uppercase and lowercase letters. This is the most expedient way to note two levels of experience, two levels of consciousness, two distinct levels of the *Mind*. There is no way to even begin to appreciate what is occurring in the experience of our lives without understanding this distinction.

Uppercase *Mind* is an all-encompassing *Consciousness* that contains the totality of your experience of being in this world. It comprises both the *Truth* of *Who You Are* (the part you are usually unaware of) as well as the illusional self you mistakenly assume yourself to be (the part you usually live from). This uppercase *Mind* is not where you live, but it is where *Truth* resides. It *is Truth.*

Lowercase "mind," on the other hand, is the seat of your ongoing personal, everyday experience. Fundamentally, it is the "me" you think you are. This mind determines every facet—large and small—of the experience of that "me." This includes every delusional thought you have of who you are, as well as any inkling of experience you may ever have that touches something of the *Truth* beyond that illusional "me": *Who You Are in Truth.*

In your everyday life, you experience two different parts of this lowercase mind, two different minds, if you will. These two minds determine how you attribute meaning to what you encounter. Each provides the means by which you process life. One of those minds is aligned with *Truth,* and the other defies it. This second mind is illusional; in fact, it is delusional. Sometimes, you align with *Truth,* and at other times, you deny it. That movement back and forth between these two minds constitutes your life experience, driven by your **Changing Minds**.

You might think of the presence of two minds as the presence of two selves: a "me" that is *True* and a "me" that is illusional. It is essential to understand that in any given moment, you can operate out of only one mind at a time: either the *mind* aligned with *Truth* or the mind denying it. And it is important to note that some aspect of our Being is constantly choosing between these two options. That choice, that decision you are constantly making between them, is the focus of this book.

Paradoxically, in **Changing Minds**, you are exercising a choice that does not exist in *Reality.* For how can you choose something that is not real? You can believe you are choosing between *Truth* and illusion—which is exactly what you believe you *are* doing. That is the ongoing experience of your life.

Therefore, that is where you have to start, working with that choice you *believe* you have: the choice between the aforementioned minds, between *Truth* and illusion.

The choice between *Truth* and illusion reflects the existence of two selves with which you can identify at any moment in time, two possible selves that produce two different experiences. One *Self* is associated with choosing *Truth* and has but one mission: to completely *Awaken* to *Truth*. This is a *Process* accomplished by more deeply and consistently opening to the *Truth* that *Self* knows to be real. The other self, the delusional self, has a parallel mission, but one with finite and self-serving goals: to manage its conflictual existence in this world. It accomplishes its goal through the justification and rationalization of all of its choices.

Throughout the hours and days and years of your life, you are always engaged in **Changing Minds**, making that single choice between *Truth* and illusion. Which "self" will you identify with, and what experience will that produce? It is not hard to see that the *Self* identified with *Truth* will lead to an experience that is different in every way from the experience brought on by the self-denying *Truth*. Admittedly, it does not feel like you choose your experience as you go through your life. Instead, it feels more as if life hands you an infinite array of choices that lead to outcomes and experiences beyond your control.

Changing Minds is about learning that in the end, there is only one choice to make, and it is not "how do you respond to whatever is happening in the present moment?" but rather which mind will you operate from to experience it? For once you have chosen a mind, there are no further choices, no more options. The mind in denial of *Truth* will not have any choices that include relationship, *Love*, compassion, or forgiveness. The mind aligned with reality will have no choices that include separation, hatred, blame, or punishment. The options for responding are predetermined by the mind with which you have chosen to identify. For whether you choose the mind aligned with *Truth*, or the mind in denial of it, all subsequent actions will be dictated by that universe of thought.

It is like working within the framework of a computer program—once you make an initial choice for running a particular program, there are certain things you can do, certain operations you can perform, and others that are absolutely outside the realm of possibility. You are free to choose any number of operations available within that one program, but you are *not* free to choose an operation it does not contain. Let's look more closely at how this works.

Take the program that is in denial of *Truth*, the one that is illusional. The limit of this program is that you are only free to *change your mind about* anyone or anything that occurs. For example, you might see something one way in one moment, and then see it differently in the next, because you *changed your mind about* it. For some reason, you decide to see it differently. Maybe you have new information. Maybe you are consciously trying to be "better" or more "spiritual." Whatever the case, you are still operating within the context of the limits of one program, and there are serious limits. You can only move so far in this mind.

In dramatic contrast, when you C*hange Minds*, you change states of *Consciousness*. In effect, you choose to utilize an entirely different program. It is not the willful attempt to see someone or something differently. Rather, a genuine shift in *Consciousness* takes place, which makes everything different. This is not abstract. We all know what it feels like to experience such a shift in *Consciousness*: it happens when you are deeply moved by a sunset, or a piece of music, or something you read or hear someone say. That experience of "being moved" reflects a movement that actually takes place, a movement from one mind to another. Once you are "moved," new thoughts and feelings occur which simply were not there before.

Both the fields of psychology and religion are rich with examples that might help further clarify the distinction between **Changing Minds** and *changing your mind about* something. Both psychology and religion attempt to lead us to think differently about ourselves, to *change our minds about* ourselves, our thoughts and our deeds. Both attend to how we should act in this world and how our choices shape what happens. This book in no way minimizes the potential impact or the fundamental necessity of addressing issues such as these. We *do* need to work with our minds in that way.

Moreover, psychology and religion carry the seeds of **Changing Minds** because they introduce the idea of an alternative to what we already believe, to how we are already conducting our lives. The problem, however, is that for the most part, these domains tend to leave it there, focusing only on changing behavior. *Changing my mind about* something takes center stage, precluding the real transforming experience of **Changing Minds**.

It has been our professional experience that far too much psychological work is done at and limited to the level of *changing your mind about* something. In the field of psychology, there is a great deal of interest in first helping someone identify ways he might be thinking about some presenting problems, and then helping him discover alternative, more effective, ways to think about those problems.

Helping someone learn how to *change his mind about* something might be the most beneficial approach with particular individuals or in certain situations. Those specific clients may desperately need some measure of psychological relief, some hope for remedy. But in the end, the assumed "gain" may be the mere illusion of change, because nothing has fundamentally been altered. The client has not learned to *Change Minds*, to shift his *Consciousness* so that he can experience his life differently. The result is that his experience will continue to be some form of the same.

If a problem is only addressed at a more elemental level, solely within the frame of reference of one mind, the source of what is actually creating the distress has not been attended to. For instance, this could be the client's belief that he is lacking, weak, or defective. As long as he only *changes his mind about* the problem, that underlying belief will be maintained at a deeper level in his unconscious. Chances are, any experience of relief that comes from his sense of resolution will only be temporary, and that underlying belief will eventually return to confound him in another form. In falling for the "gains" he experiences when he *changes his mind about* something, he may ultimately discover that all he really did was postpone, and ironically, interfere with, the *Process* of true resolution or healing.

For example, a couple may seek psychotherapy as a means of working through issues they are struggling with in their marriage. In doing so, they might find a therapeutic course of action extremely valuable. In fact, the net result of their having learned how to *change their minds about* each other and their issues might be to avoid divorce. And the couple should be applauded for such efforts. This work in no way questions the power or validity of *changing our minds about* things. But **Changing Minds** adds an entirely different and significantly more important dimension to the experience.

The couple may have *changed their minds about* issues that allowed them to circumvent a divorce, but in their having merely *changed their minds about* their problems, has the experience of their relationship radically altered? To put it more bluntly, did the experience of resolving some issues lead to their profound realization of *Love*, their love for each other, or did it merely change behaviors that prevented divorce?

Likewise, with regard to religion, far too many of its tenets remain fixed within the context of *changing our minds about* something. The emphasis is on behavior, such as refraining from certain behaviors or performing certain ritual acts. But what is ultimately accomplished if all we do is follow religious guidelines and adhere to certain proscriptions? We may have the experience of feeling "good" and of belonging to a community, but does life not look and feel pretty much the same? Has anything fundamentally been altered?

To *change your mind about* something in the context of religion may offer something similar to the experience found in the context of psychotherapy. You may feel as if you have somehow escaped the consequences of who you have been or what you have done. The fear and unworthiness driving lower levels of consciousness are powerful and disruptive motivators. They compel us to seek answers in that broad spectrum of thinking and behavior known as "relief," no matter how temporary. And unfortunately, at those lower levels, mere remedy or trying to "do it right" or "be accepted" often seems to be enough.

But relief or escape is not the same as transformation. By limiting yourself to the thinking found in that *mind*, it is possible to completely miss the radically different opportunity available when you *Change Minds*. For what you seek in religion is the

Truth of *Unconditional Love,* and that is not possible if you do not *Change Minds.*

Unfortunately, on a global level, very few of us are aware of the possibility of something beyond *changing our minds about* something. We are so desperate for release from our pain and suffering that mere relief can seem wondrous—and we settle for that. But in religion as well as in psychotherapy, relief is not the same as genuine resolution. Seeming to escape the consequences for who we believe we are, to somehow believe we have found a way to be acquitted for our "crimes," is not the same as the recognition of *Who We Are in Truth.*

We reiterate that *changing your mind about* something can be an essential part of the process of **Changing Minds.** *Changing your mind about* an idea, a person, an event, can be a manifestation of your personal evolution. It can represent a genuine effort to evolve and grow. It can even be indicative of a refusal to remain imprisoned by your historical conditioning, that is, the way you were brought up or the way you have always done things in the past. As you do so, you will experience relief, you may even evolve—but there are limits to that evolution.

What adds another dimension to that evolution in *Consciousness* is the increasing recognition that you can choose to *Change Minds,* which you gradually learn will bring with it an entirely different order of experience. It is this new order of experience, this glimpse of the possibility of something more, the promise of the real treasure possible, that keeps you moving forward. You find yourself willing to challenge everything that stands in the way, and eager to advance on your *Journey.*

2

The Paradoxical Journey

"How wonderful that we have met with a paradox. Now we have some hope of making progress." Niels Bohr

Many have compared the course of our lives to a journey. For us, from birth to death, this is a *Journey* from the darkness of unconsciousness towards the light of *Consciousness*, to what we are calling *Awakening*.

For too long, we have existed within the darkness of unconsciousness. Unconsciousness is at one end of the spectrum of *Consciousness*. It is the result of having fallen asleep to what it *True*, which means we are then operating with distorted thinking and a confused *mind*. Unconsciousness is barely in touch with *Reality*—if at all. You probably know exactly what we are speaking of: that persistent uneasiness that creeps up from time to time to remind you that you do not know what you are doing here—or why. Or perhaps in your life, it is an awareness that your current understanding is not all there is, but you do not know where else to look, what else to do, how else to *be*. And this is just the outermost layer of unconsciousness.

At the other end of the spectrum, *Awakening* is rousing yourself from the slumber induced by the human condition to *Truth*. *Awakening* necessarily includes an awareness of the *Reality* of what is occurring in your life, what your life is really about, and of course, the *Reality* of *Who You Are in Truth*.

There are multiple levels to the idea that the *Journey* is *paradoxical*. Perhaps the most superficial level is that as we move through life, we fundamentally know what is true, but very often live from what is not. Worse yet, we do not even seek to align with *Truth*. Instead, our efforts are more likely directed toward distorting *Truth* to whatever our need may be in the moment. This tendency certainly drives much of our lives. It dictates how we think and the way we act. We assess our lives from a delusional point of view and then attempt to solve our problems in ways that can only be described as equally delusional. The result is that as we manage our lives in this way, we seriously distort *Truth*. Sometimes, we altogether forget what *Truth* looks like.

It is also *paradoxical* to note that despite the lies we accept as truth and the illusions we live by to convince ourselves that our daily lives "work," nothing alters the intrinsic and unchangeable nature of *Who We Are in Truth*. *Truth* exists independent of everything we do or have ever done. This is in stark, and sometimes terrifying, contrast to the guilt/shame/unworthiness every one of us believes we are and works so hard to hide.

Our *True Nature* is unalterable and is founded on *Innocence*. This does not mean our actions are insignificant, or that we are not totally accountable for them. It does, however, mean that we can be, in fact, that we *are* loved in spite of them.

Calling ourselves "guilty" or "shameful" or "unworthy" does not make it so in *Truth*. Abraham Lincoln is said to have asked: "How many legs does a dog have if you call the tail a leg? Four. Calling a tail a leg doesn't make it a leg." *Truth* is true, regardless of what you call it or try to do to change it.

Since the beginning of time, man has grappled with his humanity. Despite our personal histories and various points of view, we are all looking for answers to the questions of what it means to be human, what it means to be born into and grow up in this world. How do we meet the challenge of mastering day-to-day living in this world? The crux of the dilemma is contained in the question of "Who or what am I?" What does it mean to be a "self," or as we think of it in a more personally possessive way, what does it mean to be *my* "self?"

The *Journey* is also *paradoxical* because the nature of your experience of being in this world is paradoxical. There are two diametrically opposed ways to view your "self:" the *Self* you are in *Truth*, and the "self" you think you are. These are based upon two thought systems which lead to two entirely different universes of thought, feeling, being. The net result is that you must constantly choose between two entirely different "selves."

The *paradox* also refers to the dilemma of figuring out how both "selves" can seemingly be true. For example, how can you be loving and forgiving in the midst of war? Or how can you feel compassion for the person who grievously wronged you? The challenge is learning to acknowledge the reality of what is happening here in this world (illness, divorce, loss, etc.) without being bound to the world as the source that determines your experience. You are not always able to change what is happening, but it is always possible to choose how you are going to experience it.

Of course, the ultimate *paradox* is our belief in the possibility that there is something other than *Truth*. How could there be an alternative to *Truth*? What could that be? How could we change what is *True*? While such questions might seem absurd, that is exactly what we believe we have done. We think we have changed the unchangeable nature of *Who We Are in Truth*.

It is vital to understand that higher spiritual principles do not involve denial or encourage illusion. What they do is remind us that there is something more. They move us beyond the confines of our physical, psychological existence to a higher level of *Consciousness*. We begin to appreciate that the *Reality* of *Love* or *Oneness* or *Forgiveness* is not only possible in all circumstances, it is *Who We Are in Truth*. And we long to remember that *Truth*.

Higher order principles do not address a problem at the level on which the problem was created. They bring forth solutions that lower order principles cannot provide, and in fact, would tell us are impossible. How else can we explain parents forgiving the man who murdered their child? Or the spouse who forgives his partner's infidelity? Or a man like Nelson Mandela, who was convicted of seditious activities and sentenced to prison for 27 years. He later became President of South Africa from 1994-1999, whose ultimate freedom was not being able to walk away from 27 years in prison, but in being able to do so without bitterness and a desire for revenge?

We invite you to read this book with an open mind. Some of the ideas expressed in it may seem to conflict with your background or your beliefs. Do not impulsively use that as an excuse to reject the ideas out of hand. Make allowance for whatever measure of discomfort these new ideas might produce. Make room for something that could address the inexplicable discontent in your life, the suspicion you have about the futility of how you currently think about and live your life. Begin the *Journey* with the genuine desire to know more.

We are in no way trying to persuade you to believe something just because we believe it. We ask only that you be open-minded and curious, that you entertain these new ideas and see where they take you. And we ask that you "empty your cup." Have you ever tried to pour more liquid into a cup that is already full? There is no room for anything more. In like manner, you cannot learn what you think you already know. You may need to "empty your cup" just a little, remove some of the prejudices and preconceptions that now fill it to create space for something more.

We invite you on a *Journey* to greater understanding, along a path that leads to higher *Consciousness*. And you have to begin where you are—*exactly* where you are. Think of the locks on a canal. If you have never had the opportunity to navigate between two bodies of water at very different levels, you may not fully appreciate the time and effort such navigation requires. That task is neither fast nor easy. As you navigate from a lower body of water to a higher one, you are obliged to pass through a series of locks in order to gradually reach your destination. Such it is with *Consciousness*—passing through mental locks that lead from lower orders of understanding to higher and higher ones. The destination—that of *Awakening*—makes all the effort worthwhile.

While you are in each lock, it is easy to believe the current water level is the true level of water, because that is your experience at the moment, and it *is* the level at which your craft currently floats. Thus, you are exactly where you have to be and where you have to navigate from. As you proceed, however, you will find further locks to negotiate, each one adding to the current water level in order to slowly adjust to the level of the next higher lock. But remember, regardless of where you are in the locks, and what your present experience of water levels might be, *you* do not determine *Reality*, that is, the true level of water.   This book can and will lead you to a different, higher level of understanding. It will support your quest for clarity and *Truth*. It will assist you in unraveling the paradox of the *Journey*. It can be a guide to help you navigate through the various locks of *Consciousness* as you move towards the destination of *Awakening*. Its express purpose, then, is to raise *Consciousness*—one lock at a time.

3

Recognition

"Nature uses only the longest threads to weave her patterns, so that each small piece of her fabric reveals the organization of the entire tapestry." Richard P. Feynman

    A core assumption underlying the title of this trilogy is that we cannot change something until we first identify it. Hence, the theme of this first book is **Recognition**. Without this critical first step, we merely chase our tails in circles, aimlessly attempting to resolve misperceived problems that can only lead to false resolutions. What creates this unfortunate scenario is our fundamental cluelessness about *Who We Are in Truth* and how life actually works. **Recognition** addresses this predicament.

    We must begin with the idea of *Consciousness*, not our individual perspective on life, but rather the expanded *Awareness* in which our individual perspective exists. This leads directly to the *Mind*. We view the *Mind* from a very different perspective than most other philosophical approaches, and this is part of what makes our take on it unique. The *Mind* we speak of and direct your attention to is difficult to grasp because it cannot adequately be explained; it can only be experienced or in a sense, "witnessed." This *Mind* is the "big picture" that contains the entirety of all we know and experience in the human condition. The simple glimpses each of us has had of this *Mind* is what inspires us to undertake this *Journey of Awakening*. And it is the only force strong enough to motivate us to continue down its path.

Fundamentally, our lives are about a *Journey of Awakening* which takes us through the *Mind*. It is a *Journey* through everything we believe, everything we think, everything we think we know, everything we hold as true. This *Journey* dictates the entirety of our experience of life, for in the end, our experience is completely dependent on what we make up about it. Life is not a succession of events, but rather a stream of interpretations we call experience. There are no exceptions to this.

This *Journey of Awakening* should be accompanied with a warning label that informs each traveler that the very act of challenging what we hold to be true about ourselves and our world will inevitably be experienced as disruptive. Moreover, if seriously undertaken, the *Journey* may, at times, be experienced as utterly frightening. How could it be otherwise if we consciously take on the possibility that we do not really know who we are, or what we are doing?

Allow us to pose a basic question here at the start. Who among us is completely satisfied with himself and his experience of life? Some vague **Recognition** that we do not have the answers, that indeed, we might be wrong about what we think we know could then be the first opening. What if we discovered that the real problem we face is nothing more than our limited ideas about who we *believe* we are, our mistaken notions about what we think is happening in this world? Wouldn't it be a relief to free ourselves from our delusions and wake up to what is *True*?

Einstein famously said: "We cannot solve our problems with the same thinking we used when we created them." Another way to understand this is to suggest he was alluding to our lack of awareness of the *Mind*. We do not understand that our problems are created by what we think, by how we interpret what happens in our lives. Without even a modicum of genuine *Awareness*, all our attempts at problem-solving are doomed. Via Einstein's insight, we must find new thinking to solve old problems, or we will wind up exactly where we started.

We address this issue by raising awareness, by creating a framework through which to view the *Mind*, and thus, our life experience. We do so in this book through the exploration of such topics as: Parallel Universes, dual natures, Consciousness/unconsciousness, Mind/mind, Truth vs. illusion, Form vs. Content, Cause and Effect. It is only through the utilization of this new framework that the *real* problem can be brought clearly into view, and then honestly resolved.

Let us place this first book in the context of the entire trilogy. Book I is about the **Recognition** of the real problem we face. Once that takes place, we move to Book II, the second aspect of the *Process*: **Relinquishment**. **Relinquishment** presupposes that through the process of **Recognition**, we have a much better idea about what our real problem is, which leaves us in a significantly better position to solve that problem. This is fundamentally accomplished through our willingness to *Relinquish* anything that stands in the way of *Truth*.

The "very poor man" in the opening parable thought his problems were about money and could therefore be solved with the acquisition of a priceless pearl. He came to realize that the previously unknown ability to *give up* the pearl was the priceless treasure he sought. Like the "very poor man," **Relinquishment** leads us to challenge our unconscious, unquestioned conviction that what we believe about our lives is true, so that what *is True* becomes available to us to be seen, known, and experienced.

The *Process* that leads to **Relinquishment** is a gradual *Awakening*. It is the evolution of *Truth* in the *Mind* as we come out of the slumber induced by the thinking that constitutes the human condition. We become increasingly willing to *Relinquish* those beliefs that keep us spellbound and limited, anything that would hinder the restoration of *Truth* to the *Mind*.

In Book II, we move from a more global framework of theorizing, to exploring how *Consciousness* plays out on a personal level. This includes such ideas as the illusion of choice, sacrifice and loss, attachment, and the psychological dynamics of denial, projection, and dissociation. We also make note of all of the activities in our minds that cloud our thinking, such as management, coping, busyness, and distractions.

Relinquishment is about surrendering what we cling to in our lives instead of the *Truth*. This is accompanied by a growing awareness that such a surrender is not the act of sacrifice we assumed it would be. As we challenge what stands in the way of our *Awakening*, we increasingly sense the liberation it brings. We realize that we do not create *Truth*; rather, we remove the obstacles that block our awareness of *It*. With the **Relinquishment** of illusions, *Truth* is restored, for *Truth* is all that is left in the *Mind*.

Understanding what must be *Relinquished*, we are at last ready to explore the elements of the *Practice* that facilitates and deepens the *Process* of **Restoration**. The focus of **Restoration** is the development of a *Practice*. **Restoration** of *Truth* is the ultimate purpose of this work. Book III, **Restoration**, includes learning about and incorporating such principles as authentic choice, forgiveness, mindfulness, stillness, guidance, dedication, devotion, and relationship.

Our *Journey of Awakening* rests on two core constructs. One is *Mind*, which is the primary backdrop of the first two books. *Mind* is where the *Journey* takes place. The second is *Process*, which is manifest in the development of a *Practice*, and is the focus of the third book. *Process* is how we advance on the *Journey*. Life is not static. It is pure *Process*. It is ever evolving. We advance in this *Process* in direct proportion to our willingness to challenge all that is not *True* and embrace what is *True*.

Let us conclude this chapter by clearly stating our purpose. We are not asking you to *change your mind about* anything. We are not trying to convince you to believe what we believe. We are certainly not asking you to blindly accept what we are saying is true. We are not in charge of what is *True*, and neither are you. *Truth* cannot be described or explained. *Truth* is ineffable and must be *experienced*. We cannot tell you what is *True*, but we can certainly point towards where it can be discovered.

A sensei once told his student that as he points his finger up towards the heavens, he is directing his student's attention to something up there to behold, to *experience*. But if the student focuses only on the pointing finger, he will miss the entire celestial panorama. Likewise, it is not what we say in these books that matters, but what we are pointing to. We extend to you an invitation to join us, to look to where we are pointing, to discover what is *True*.

4

The Bear and the Reindeer

"In short, not only are things not what they seem, they are not even what they are called!" Francisco de Quevedo

The ideas expressed in our trilogy will be transformational for many readers because they represent a philosophical depth that, when grasped, cannot help but alter the way they think. These ideas will necessarily challenge your unconscious notions of "how things are," and even "why things are." It is quite likely they will therefore be accompanied by some vague degree of threat, for what you have believed until now is how you have held the world together. But do not let this deter you. For while these new ideas are to be taken seriously, they are not intended to be daunting.

We would like to introduce here at the outset a lighter, novel approach to understanding what we are saying. Such an approach serves two purposes. The first is to bring a sense of levity to this otherwise serious exploration. After all, the ultimate outcome of our *Journey* is genuine freedom and the joy that accompanies it.

The second purpose of such a novel approach is to bypass our natural tendency to word-associate, that is, to assume we know what is being talked about because of the specific choice of words used. Part of the problem we have with tackling concepts like "consciousness" or "ego" or "spirit," for example, is that the previous associations and identifications we have all attached to these and other key words will interfere with the possibility of entertaining new understanding, new meanings.

It is a truism that when any one of us encounters a word like "joy" or "guilt" or "condemnation," we automatically think we know what that word means—because we *do* know what that word means to us in the context of our personal history and life experience. The word "freedom," to take but one example, does not mean the same thing to an American citizen as it does to a citizen of Afghanistan. Americans are born with an idea of "freedom" and often take it for granted, while "freedom" may be a completely different concept to someone in another country—and something he must fight for.

So from the start, we are using all kinds of terms—and most of the terms themselves are not new—in our exploration that are quite likely to stir up different feelings in people, depending on their backgrounds, education, experience, and present willingness to learn. There is always the potential problem that any word we use such as "*Mind*" or "mind," "*Consciousness*" or "unconsciousness," "*Spirit*" or "ego," will evoke an immediate response in your mind that could make you assume you know what we are talking about. And once you make such an assumption, it may create controversy in your mind, increasing the likelihood that you will become at odds with the message we are trying to convey. The invitation we extend to you would be *not* to assume you already know what we are talking about. We wholeheartedly encourage you to keep an open mind and just be willing to explore with us.

We propose to bypass this process of habitual word association by introducing two new words whose previous associations are unlikely to interfere: the Bear and the Reindeer. Bear with us here. The idea of the Bear and the Reindeer has its origins in an experience that Frank had when he was in kindergarten. He was assigned the role of a reindeer in the kindergarten Christmas play. Our Mother spent a great deal of time creating and sewing a brown reindeer suit that covered his whole body like a very loose skin diver's suit. She even managed to create antlers out of wire and padding that were attached to his head via a tight-fitting brown hood. The only part of him that showed in this overall brown costume was his unhappy little face.

There is a photo of him standing with his sister, Kathy, in her princess outfit for the same play in front of their house in New Orleans. While Kathy is smiling her delighted princess smile, there is no mistaking the look of mortification on Frank's face. At a glance, one sees the brown reindeer and then notices that the face of the reindeer is a little human being who is embarrassed beyond words and does not begin to know how to process what is going on. The resulting Bear/Reindeer concept came into being many years later as Frank and Kathy in their therapy practices recognized the "costumes" we wear that hide or disguise the *Truth of Who We Are*.

Instead of using terms such as "Spirit" and "ego," which are loaded with all kinds of positive and negative associations, from here on, we will use the terms "Bear" and "Reindeer" to point towards those areas of *Consciousness* with which we are working. In fact, it is very useful to think of us human beings as having a split in our *Consciousness*—a split which results in two very distinct domains of being. One domain is aligned with *Spirit* and *Truth*, and we will call that "Bear." The other domain, aligned with ego, is delusional. Worse, it is a lie. This domain we will call "Reindeer." This division of *Consciousness* into two domains is just a starting place for the work we have to do.

In line with the lighter side of this presentation method, this whole idea of the split in *Consciousness*, the distinction between *Spirit* and ego, *Truth* and illusion, took an interesting twist in the form of a stuffed animal. Picture this: a stuffed animal that, for the most part, looks like a cute little brown reindeer. It has brown fur, brown paws, a brown scalp with ears, and fuzzy-looking reindeer antlers. It pretty much looks like a reindeer. The odd thing about it though, is that it has a distinctly different, cream-colored face. On closer inspection, the cream-colored face is definitely not that of a reindeer, but rather that of a bear. Yet further scrutiny reveals this is not a reindeer at all, but rather a bear in a reindeer costume. It becomes apparent the reindeer scalp, reindeer ears, and reindeer antlers are nothing more than a hood that has been pulled up and over the bear's head to hide or disguise him. Thus, this stuffed animal became an amazing prop in our work.

Let us bring you up to date on our costumed friend. Frank always hated (and hid) that kindergarten picture of himself in the reindeer suit, but several years ago, Kathy decided it would be great fun to remind him of it anyway. She began to find and give him lots of different small bears—all sorts of incredibly cute bears in reindeer and various other costumes. Imagine a little bear face in a green Christmas tree costume, or in a white bunny suit with floppy pink ears. The point we are making is that it was always a bear that assumed many disguises in all kinds of different costumes, all of which hid the truth of its true identity. By the way, Frank's response was consistently "Oh no!" but he always smiled—and even laughed at himself with the rest of us.

If we look a little more closely at what we are introducing with this idea of the bear in various costumes, we are stating that the *Truth* is always bear, and never the costume that makes him appear to be something else. This little stuffed animal highlights the idea that although at first glance we may *look* like we are reindeers dressed up in human costumes), the *Truth* is we are always Bears (*Spirit* inside the costume).

This model affords us uncomplicated access to a number of ideas related to our thesis. These include understanding the difference between *Spirit* and ego, *Truth* and illusion, Bear and Reindeer, costume and reality. It points towards the fact that we are *not* fighting against something (a costume) to determine our reality; our *Reality* always *is*. Nor are we fighting against an imagined Reindeer to *claim* we are Bears. What is happening is that we have too long identified falsely with our Reindeer costumes and we are now waking up to, remembering, the *Truth* of *Who We Are* as Bears.

That is the purpose of this series: to *Recognize* the scam the Reindeer costume (ego) presents, *Relinquish* the thinking that holds it in place, and be *Restored* to our *True* identity as Bear *(Spirit)*.

5

The Reindeer with a "Halo"

"We are so used to disguising ourselves to others that we end by disguising ourselves from ourselves." François VI, Duc de la Rochefoucauld

Let us take a quick detour in the current discussion to make one further distinction in our premise. In general, we assume the anxiety and generalized tension we humans feel can only be the result of the Bear and the Reindeer being always at odds, at war with each other. Nothing could be further from the truth. The discomfort we experience is contained solely within the mind of the Reindeer. This is because the two universes of Bear and Reindeer are independent of each other and therefore, cannot be at odds. Their independence from each other is complete.

The conflict we are referring to is caused by an odd sort of twist, which exists solely in the Reindeer mind. The oddity is that this split is actually between what we are going to call a "full-fledged" Reindeer, and a **Reindeer with a "Halo."** This means that entirely within the universe of the Reindeer, there is part of that mind that completely embodies the principles of the ego. This is the "full-fledged" Reindeer. At the same time, there is another part of that same mind that is a Reindeer *pretending* that it is a Bear. This is where many of us live, and we are calling this a *Reindeer with a "Halo."*

The "full-fledged" Reindeer is fairly easy to recognize. It experiences life as if it were at odds with everything, and always vulnerable to, and a victim of, what is occurring in the world. It is always out to win, to be right, to survive. When we are angry or cruel or impatient or at odds with anything that is occurring in our lives, we are this "full-fledged" Reindeer. This is not a foreign concept to any of us—in thought or in practice.

The *Reindeer with a "Halo"* is an entirely different animal. It is much more subtle, slippery, and surprisingly unconscious to us. The *Reindeer with a "Halo"* is so labeled because it gives the *appearance* of acting like the Bear. It looks like it is being generous when in reality, it is only seeking to win bonus points for its behavior. It may exhibit patience or compassion, when what it is really doing is withholding its true feelings, putting on a good show—either out of fear or because doing so gets it something it wants more than authentic expression in that moment.

The *Reindeer with a "Halo"* appears to get away with what it is doing because of the profound confusion between *Form*—the *appearance* of what is happening—and *Content*—the *meaning* we ascribe to what is happening (refer to later Chapters 11, 12, and 13 for a deeper examination of *Form and Content*). For example, two individuals could both perform the same act in *Form*, such as make a large donation to a charity or to a religious organization, but the *Content* could be radically different. One person could give the money based on a deep belief in the cause, while the other's motivation could be a desire to be viewed as a great philanthropist or humanitarian. In both cases, the *Form* (what happened) is the same, but the *Content* (what is actually going on in the mind of the donor) is obviously and significantly different.

What the *Reindeer with a "Halo"* does in *Form* looks exactly like what the Bear would do. What is actually taking place, though, is that the Reindeer with a "Halo" is merely attempting to compensate for the "full-fledged" Reindeer in one and the same mind. The conflict or war in that one mind is not between the Bear and the Reindeer, but rather between the "full-fledged" Reindeer and the *Reindeer with a "Halo"* trying to cover up or compensate for what it is doing.

It is an ingenious device, because it allows the person in the Reindeer *mind* to believe he is not selfish, stingy, or acting solely in his own interest. This way, he can pretend (to himself) that he has all the virtues of the Bear. Unfortunately, such a ruse does not resolve anything; it merely hides the conflict.

The *"Halo"* is an ingenious device because it allows the "self" in the Reindeer mind to believe he is "good," or at least, not as "bad" as he thinks he is. But it is not really "bad," it is just his self-centered, stingy, judgmental actions that are based on the fearful ideas comprising the Reindeer thought system. The only problem is that having the pretense of the virtues of the Bear is delusional. It does not resolve the conflict in his mind, it does not resolve anything. It merely hides and postpones resolution of the real conflict, which is having chosen the wrong mind: the Reindeer mind.

6

Parallel Universes

"The range of what we think and do is limited by what we fail to notice. And because we fail to notice that we fail to notice, there is little we can do to change; until we notice how failing to notice shapes our thoughts and deeds." R. D. Laing

We now want to look at one of the new, and perhaps most difficult, ideas presented in this book: that of **Parallel Universes**, and more specifically, the simultaneity of their existence. On one level, it might appear that both the notion of *Parallel Universes* and their simultaneity would not be that difficult to grasp.

For example, it makes complete sense that two people standing side by side, watching the same event, can and do have two very different experiences of what is transpiring. Two individuals may watch the same movie and have dramatically different reactions. How is that possible? Each may describe what is happening in similar ways but have very different things to say about what it *means*. We can clearly see that these people live in two *Parallel Universes*. In each individual's universe, the experience is simply what he makes up about what is occurring. Is it good or bad, happy or sad? Each gets to ask and answer such questions in his own universe. Second by second, each one continues to have a different experience of the same event.

It is also easy to recognize that these two individuals are experiencing the same event *simultaneously*. Parallel interpretations, which lead to simultaneous *Parallel Universes* of experience in two individuals, is intuitively clear. What is far less obvious is the idea that there exist two differing, simultaneous universes within an individual psyche, that is, within each one of us. The simultaneity of experience, all within one psyche, in *Parallel Universes*, is pivotal to an understanding of the main concept of this book: **Changing Minds**. How is it possible that two *Parallel Universes* occur simultaneously within the unique psyche of one individual? What does that mean?

Consider what happens in the process of listening to a particular radio station and then selecting another channel to listen to a different one. Each radio station is playing its own program of music. Changing from one radio station to another means nothing more than that we have chosen to tune into a different program of music. Note that neither radio station's programming is based on the other's; each is completely independent.

In much the same way, as we experience life, there are *Parallel Universes* of "programming" which give way to parallel interpretations, which lead to *Parallel Universes* of experience, all within the one singular psyche of each of us. One part of our mind is processing what is occurring—that is, what is playing on one radio station—through the programming of Bear *(Spirit)*, and the other is processing what is occurring on a different radio station—through the programming of Reindeer (ego). Each program "sounds different" and leads to radically different interpretations, and therefore completely different experiences, of what is occurring; but note that each remains absolutely independent of the other. It is always our choice which radio station to tune into.

We might naïvely hope or want to believe the two universes of Bear and Reindeer will eventually converge, or that they could somehow be combined and integrated. This is not just a misunderstanding of the two, but a grave mistake. Think of the cacophony that would result from any attempt to blend two different radio stations playing different music programs. Even if it were possible, the result would be absurd.

Let's go back to the two people standing side by side. The experience of each of the two is not based on what the other one is feeling. They are each using the unique lens of who they are—that is, their personal history, their ideas and beliefs, their expectations, etc., to interpret what they see. For example, both individuals may witness the same tragic event. One might be filled with anger directed towards the one responsible for the tragedy, while the other might be filled with compassion for the suffering of everyone involved. Each independently processes the same event and *chooses* his own experience. But the experience of one in no way influences or changes the experience of the other.

We do not mean to suggest there is anything wrong with the way that either individual experiences the specifics of any given event. There is no "should" about experience. The opportunity is there, however, to look at *why* each one sees it the way he does. The choice for the source of experience is critical. Within the context of an individual psyche, one is always listening to the programming of one or the other of two "radio stations:" Bear or Reindeer. The goal then becomes to heighten our awareness of our personal choice of which radio station we *want* to listen to—that is, which thought system we will use to process what is occurring. Then, and only then, can we *Change Minds*.

Let's move to the heart of the paradox. **Changing Minds** and *changing my mind about* something occur in two *Parallel Universes*, each of which is separate, complete, and impenetrable to the other. Each is self-enclosed, internally consistent, and bound by the laws that establish it, that is, each is true within the limits of itself. Nothing can be experienced, determined, or interpreted except by the laws and principles that govern that single universe.

The problem, of course, is that one of the universes is not *True*. It may be hard to think in these terms, because we are processing everything we know through the context of one universe—the one we are unconsciously accustomed to, and the wrong one. To try to imagine "something else" (another universe) challenges us to move outside the unquestioned agreement that *this* universe is "true." Suddenly, what was "true" before cannot withstand the challenge, and another reality is established.

Perhaps you are familiar with the Swiss psychologist, Jean Piaget, who designed an experiment called the "water jar task." In this experiment, a child is presented with two glasses of different sizes with an identical volume of liquid in each. The child is then asked if the tall, slim glass contains more, less, or the same amount of liquid as the short, wide glass. Before a child has acquired the concept known as the "conservation of liquid quantity," she will always say the taller glass contains more liquid. The interpretation of the events is completely consistent and "correct" within the context of that child's universe at that moment in development. This is "true" in the unidimensional universe of her understanding at that age, but it is not *True*.

The point we are trying to make is that something may be "real"—until it is no longer "real" in our experience. We would ask that you be willing to challenge what you now believe is "real," examine what you think "contains" your current experience, and question your accepted ideas about *how* the mind works.

7

Characteristics of the Parallel Universes

"Your problem is how you are going to spend this one odd and precious life you have been issued. Whether you're going to spend it trying to look good and creating the illusion that you have power over people and circumstances, or whether you are going to taste it, enjoy it and find out the truth about who you are." Anne Lamott

We spoke of the concept of "conservation of liquid volume" in the Piaget experiment. Let's look at the abstract idea of "conservation" in each of the *Parallel Universes*. In the Reindeer universe, we are in the universe composed of space and time, where there are objects, forms, and people, each one separated from the others. If I have a cup of water and I choose to give it to you, I no longer have the water, you do. I share the water with you by giving it to you, but as soon as I hand it to you, I no longer have it.

In the Bear universe, we enter a universe that is abstract and formless, where sharing takes on an entirely different meaning. In that universe, sharing is not an event that occurs *between* objects, with a distinct giver and receiver. In the Bear universe, when I share an idea with you, we both have the idea. In fact, my idea is strengthened and enlarged by sharing it with you. I now have more, not less, than I did before I shared it. This is the true meaning of sharing. We share our ideas with you through the writing of this book. As you read it, nothing is lost in the process. Quite the contrary, our shared ideas have grow

The Reindeer universe is based on separation: that world consists of distinct things, people, places, all of which are separated by time and space. The Bear universe, on the other hand, transcends the notion of separation and leads to a unified perception and experience of being in the world.

On the most elementary level, each of us is a separate, distinct human being, but there is something that transcends this distinct human being, this "me," and that is my humanity, which is shared with everyone on the planet. We each have unique experiences, families, histories, and we occupy different physical locations on the planet, but we share our humanity: we got here the same way, we learn, and we grow in the same way. And though there may be striking distinctions even on this level, we are all humans. We are all doing the same thing: figuring it out as we go.

In the Reindeer universe, life is about survival, which means each of us is at odds with everyone else in the universe. If two of us are dying of thirst, only one of us drinks whatever water exists—and the other dies. It is a tightly wound thought system from which there is no escape, because it *is* what is true at that level. It is important to emphasize we are not denying this. If I don't get the water, I *will* die. But my being at odds with everyone and everything is what produces the tension and suffering I feel. We fight over the same piece of land, the same job, the same partner—because only one of us can have it. We fight over one idea, one belief, one philosophy, because we think only one of us can be right. It is a fear-based stance with a "me" against everything else, the elements, aging and time, the extra dollar—"me" against all of it.

In the Bear universe, there is an evolution taking place, where I am moving out of the more primitive "me against you" stance toward the increasing recognition of a higher order. This is not a genuine evolution of thinking, but rather a growing recognition of what is *True* by the gradual removal of everything that is *not* true. In one universe, it could be said the brain is the master that tries to figure things out and win, survive. In the other universe, it could be said the *Mind*—which is not the same thing as the brain—is in charge, and seeks only to know what is *True*.

The very act of writing this book reflects that same process. It is an attempt to conceptualize and articulate experience—which we acknowledge cannot in fact be done. Developmentally, we have not yet awakened to the point where we are able to understand anything other than the "reality" that it looks like there is more water in the tall, slim glass, and that there seem to be more benefits to being a Reindeer than a Bear. *Truth* cannot be substantiated in the Reindeer universe, because we are like the child choosing between the tall, slim glass and the short, fat glass of water. But we persist because we have some sense that there is "more"—more to learn, more to know, more to experience.

What is *True* often does not make sense in the Reindeer universe, where we live most of the time. In the end, there can be no other pathway to *Truth* but our *real* experience of it. This is not necessarily a conscious process. More often, it occurs as simple moments of realization, the recognition that what you thought was true can no longer contain your experience. Perhaps you remember a time when you said: "I can't believe that..." because you were sure "that" meant something else. It always *had* meant "that," but suddenly, that definition no longer works. Stop a minute now and go back to that experience. What was your experience of "before" and "after?" *What* happened and *how* did that happen?

You may recall some event, some way you experienced something in your life that defied what you thought you believed until that very moment. Perhaps you were touched by something unexpectedly lovely or innocent, or maybe you witnessed an act of forgiveness for someone who did not "deserve" it. There was something that moved you in a way that took you by surprise, and you struggled to make it "fit" in the whole thought system you believed to be true—until that very moment. But it did not fit, and your choice was either to deny the *Truth* of your experience, tamper with the evidence (we will discuss this in greater detail in the chapter on *Form and Content),* or make more space in your mind for something else—something *more.* We would suggest you did not "*change your mind about*" that something; rather, you *Changed Minds.*

We are not proposing anything truly new. What we *are* doing is illuminating the dynamics of our personal human experience in a way that hopefully stimulates your desire to know the *Truth.* Experience is experience, and impossible to articulate thoroughly. The best we can do to help you grasp all this is to point you in a new direction and facilitate your choosing to experience it from Bear.

In this context, it means something we all have and know: a collective remembering. It is our attempt to remember and to aid others in remembering. We are all in the same boat, the same paradoxical condition of being in the middle of what we call a human experience. What makes it paradoxical is that we are simultaneously "this" we are experiencing, and yet "not this" in *Truth*. Our aim is to address that paradox by looking at what is really going on, seeking to understand at a deeper level, and ultimately, remembering how to *Awaken*.

Our goal is to raise your consciousness so you become aware there *is* something else, and choose to see something different: the *Truth*, which is not up to you to create. You will come to recognize the choices of the Reindeer world are limited, so the only way you can even see the choices of the Bear world is to challenge what you now believe. This is not a guarantee of life change, but it is a guarantee of a change of experience.

A beautiful example comes from the renowned artist Michelangelo, who sculpted a series of statues known as "the Slaves." Michelangelo looked deeper into the giant slabs of marble to "see" forms imprisoned within and famously spoke of his desire to liberate them. His objective was to remove the extraneous marble around the figures so that the slaves could emerge, could be freed. But it was necessary to do the hard work of removing everything that was not relevant, everything that was *not* the slave.

This is what it means to free the Bear by challenging the Reindeer world. The slab of marble is the Reindeer world, with you as a "slave" trapped within. In challenging everything you now believe, you are able to remove what is not real and the liberated "you" emerges.

We must emulate Michelangelo and remember that it is worth it to do the hard work of aligning with *Truth* and chiseling away everything that interferes with that. It is essential to understand that anything less than dealing with the *Truth* is only shuffling reality to meet your current needs—and that cannot last.

8

The Impeccability of Each Universe

"The Greek word for truth 'aletheia' doesn't mean the opposite of falsehood. It means the opposite of 'lethe,' oblivion. Truth is what is remembered." Marilyn French

Another way to approach this dichotomy of Bear and Reindeer universes is to think of *Consciousness* as an energy. This allows us to imagine that our experience is created by the movement of this energy into one or the other of the universes of Bear or Reindeer. Think of it this way: when this energy, our *Consciousness*, moves into one of these universes, the self that occupies that universe is brought to life. That self then directs all we subsequently experience.

Remember we stated that each of the two universes of Bear and Reindeer is based on a thought system. Now let's compare those two thought systems to a computer program. A computer program is what makes sense of the data presented to it. The Reindeer thought system is the one closest to what we would consider "human being-ness," and that program is based primarily on *Form*, what is seen and heard. We rarely take into consideration the fact that the actual data is comprised of light and sound waves, which in themselves have no meaning. It is the program that processes the data, but the thought system that gives it meaning.

Several important points need to be made here. First, each of the two thought systems of Bear and Reindeer rests on solid foundations, impeccable within themselves, just as a computer program is impeccable within itself. This means that once you have chosen a universe, everything is absolutely consistent within that universe; everything makes sense in that universe.

For example, within the Reindeer universe, wrongdoing demands punishment, and betrayal leads to hatred. Within the universe of Bear, however, there is only "innocence forgotten" and no such thing as betrayal. Remember we are not talking about what occurs in the world, but rather our *experience* of what occurs. And that is a choice—not a choice about what happened or what is going to happen next, but a choice about which universe we choose to experience whatever happens.

That said, it should be clear the problem is not what one thinks or believes within either of the universes. The problem is the cornerstone on which each of the universes rests. Once that cornerstone, that core belief, is accepted, everything else that is thought or believed, becomes what is experienced as true within that universe.

The Bear universe is based on the core principle that our ultimate identity is *Innocence*. This means that our *True Innocence* cannot be destroyed—it can only be forgotten. In contrast, the Reindeer universe is based on a core principle that we are guilty, which means we have destroyed our *Innocence*, and this cannot be changed—or redeemed. If this is true, then all we can ever do is learn to cope with our guilt. Let us elaborate.

All we ever do is witness what we believe, and this is based on one of the two thought systems we have identified with: Bear or Reindeer. Each thought system is powered only by belief, and each is totally consistent within itself. Once you buy into a thought system (Bear or Reindeer), the whole world will appear consistent with that thought system—logical and unchanging.

Reassuringly, we cannot change the fact that what is *True* is *True*. *Truth* can be denied, but it cannot be changed. So if our *True Nature* is *Innocence*, then as such, it cannot be changed, and we will forever be *Innocent*. This is not of our making and exists independently of what we believe.

If we choose to deny the *Truth*, however, then there are no holds barred. In the vacuum of denial, we are free to—and we *do*—make up and believe whatever we want to. The denial of our *Innocence* leads us into a universe where guilt is what is "true." This becomes a Pandora's Box which leads to a whole different order of thought.

Guilt is a declaration that *Innocence* has, in fact, been destroyed, and is a horror with which we now have to deal. The Reindeer thought system sets into motion an elaborate means of dealing with our guilt. Guilt demands punishment and requires payment. This then generates fear as part of the payment for the wrong that has been done—fear of punishment. And of course, the Reindeer thought system offers to help us manage and cope with that fear. It is what accounts for all of the psychological defenses we use, such as denial, projection, wishful thinking, etc.

The second point to make is that, as absurd as it may seem, there is only ever one choice each of us ever makes, and that is which universe to enter, and thus, which self to identify with, and which source to use for all experience. Fundamentally, moment by moment, each of us exists as choice, a single choice. And that choice is simply between the Bear and the Reindeer. When we choose to enter one of those two universes, we occupy the self whose identity is defined there, and consequently, we have all our experience as it is defined in that universe.

A very clear example of this came up in a recent workshop where the participants were asked if they basically wanted what might generally be called the "peace of God." There was no hesitation. Everyone in the room agreed they did. Then they were instructed to monitor their states of mind throughout the following week to become acutely aware of any time they felt anger, annoyance—or even the slightest irritation. The directive to each person was to *own* at that moment the astonishing realization that "I do *not* want the peace of God." As crazy as that may seem, my "not *having* the peace of God" is a choice. It is the polar opposite of "I *do* want the peace of God."

All of us would probably proclaim that we want "the peace of God." So what accounts for the times when we are not experiencing that? In those moments, we are reserving the right to hold judgment or attack someone or ourselves. If I am not experiencing peace, "I do *not* want the peace of God." It is that simple. It is choosing between the Bear and the Reindeer, between the two universes. If I occupy the self that truly wants the peace of God, I will experience the peace of God, regardless of the situation. But to do so, I must relinquish my right to hold judgment or to attack anyone—myself included. Then, of course, if I do not want/choose the peace of God, I will not experience it.

There are laws that rule each universe. It is extremely important to note that upon making the single choice about which universe to enter, we then surrender *all* further choice, for we are am bound by the laws of the thought system that governs that universe. It is no different than choosing to go to another country where the laws are completely different than the laws the govern the United States. We are bound by the laws of that country. We are not free to disagree with them and just do as we please.

Similarly, as a human being in the physical world, we are bound by certain laws, like the law of gravity. If we choose to disagree with, or ignore that law, and step off a ten-story building, we will fall and stop suddenly a few seconds later, not because Nature is out to get us, but because it is the law of the physical universe we inhabit. If we defy the law, there are consequences. As you well know, there are also consequences for choosing not to live in peace, for denying our *Innocence*, for refusing *Love*. There will most certainly be consequences—like conflict—for those choices.

So there are two universes, resting on different foundations—one based on *Innocence*, the other based on guilt. It is fairly straightforward to ascertain the thinking produced in each universe. What makes it so straightforward is that we *live* in such thinking; we see it in operation all the time. Without even knowing we are doing so, we are always following the thinking and obeying the laws of one or other of these universes. We use them as the basis for directing all our thoughts and all our actions, like being loving or condemning, being at peace or being afraid.

No one can argue this world's thought system, that is, the Reindeer thought system, rests on a belief in right and wrong. This is why almost every facet of the world is in conflict. Every one of us believes we are right about what we believe and what we do—and that anyone (indeed, everyone) not in agreement with us, is wrong. This is what pits everyone against everyone else: individuals against individuals, groups against groups, nations against nations. In all those cases, each one believes he knows what is right and what is wrong.

What is hidden yet implicit in this entire processing though, is a fundamental belief in "right and wrong," in "innocence and guilt." Moreover, in such a system, the Right are innocent, and the Wrong are guilty. This inadvertently keeps our minds preoccupied with "right-ness" and "wrong-ness," as opposed to having even the tiniest understanding of what is really going on, what is actually *True*. Both "right" and "wrong" are in the same universe, that of the Reindeer.

This point is vitally important: both universes *cannot* be True because they are diametrically opposed. We can get to the point where we believe only one of them is true because we only experience them one at a time as we move back and forth between them. However, in *Truth*, only one of them is *True*, and our *Real Identity* can only be found in one.

It may be hard to grasp—but inescapable—that after entering either universe, there is no choice about what is true or false. What is *True* is already defined; it is established in each universe. Within the Reindeer universe, guilt is true, and all one can do is cope with that. Within the Bear universe, *Innocence* is *True*, and all one must do is *Awaken* to that. As we bridge the two worlds, it is not a question of "doing something" so we can recognize the *Truth* and have peace. It is about removing the blocks we ourselves have put in place, so we can be at peace and experience the *Truth* that is already—and always—there.

The point is to resurrect the consciousness of choice. En route, we work with the choice between the universes, that is, we choose to experience what it is like to be the self that abides in each of these universes. As we move toward *Truth*, we discover all that exists in the Reindeer universe is the *illusion* of choice.

As we evolve, we remember we can only be truly satisfied with the *Truth*. All the lies and illusions we bought into in the Reindeer universe begin to lose their appeal. Everything we have been using to quell our fears has less and less power, and gradually becomes meaningless. The *Truth* that emerges as we relinquish this is what guides us. Ultimately, we evolve to the point of realizing that not only is there is no choice at all, but that we do not even want one. It is *Awakening* to the fact that only what is *True* is *Real*, and that there is nothing else to choose.

9

Dreaming and the Dreamer

"Without change, something sleeps inside us, and seldom awakens. The sleeper must awaken." Frank Herbert

A paradox is a self-contradictory or counterintuitive statement or argument. This means some things cannot be understood or processed at the level of the mind on which they were—or are being—created. As a context within which to explore this, let's look at dreaming.

When we go to sleep at night and dream, it seems as if we access a different consciousness, a different level of mind, a different sort of awareness. Our experience is that we "put to sleep" what we would normally call our conscious mind, the mind we experience all things from when we are awake. The different level of consciousness we then enter, we call dreaming. But what actually occurs when we dream?

When we fall asleep and begin to dream, we effectively leave behind the "real" world—that is, we completely lay aside the reality that rules our experience when awake. In the absolute freedom unique to dreams, we are permitted to break all the rules that bind our waking world together. We can ignore the law of gravity and fly. We can disobey the laws of life and death, be killed and come back to life. We are free to make up reality in any way we choose. We can live in a different country, exist in a different period of time, be a member of a different family, do whatever we like. The dream figure each of us calls "me" in the dream has distinctly different liberties than the individual we experience as "me" living in this world. My "self" in this world and my "me" as a dream figure when I am asleep are two very different entities.

When we dream, we become gods in the sense that we are the creators of everything that occurs, with absolutely no limitations on the specifics of what we dream. No one is responsible for the dream but us. There is nothing that occurs outside of our control, our mind, our making. We decide the setting, the participants, the plot, the interactions, the outcomes, everything! The entire universe of the dream world occurs in one mind—*my* mind. But this is only a single aspect of what takes place when we dream.

It will be helpful to establish a further distinction between the dreamer of the dream, and myself as a dream figure in the dream. It is *I* who dreams the dream, and no one can do that for me. So there is a "me" that is the dreamer who is dreaming the dream. There is also a dream figure in the dream I identify as "me," but this "me" is clearly not the dreamer. In fact, this dream figure's experience is vastly different from that of the dreamer—although, paradoxically, *I* am both. The dreamer experiences the whole dream, while the dream figure can only experience a tiny, limited perspective: that of a singular, bodily figure I identify as myself in the dream. The figure in the dream has no awareness of the dreamer of the dream. This distinction will become increasingly significant as we go along.

Upon awakening, most of us are at least partially aware we dreamed the dream, and we can simultaneously experience (if only in moments) the dream itself through that single dream figure we thought of as ourselves. We may wake up in a sweat and look around to be sure we are safe from the threat in the dream. Or we may wake up with a big smile, only to realize the source of that happiness is not present, not even real.

We want to emphasize the unmistakable difference in experience between these two "selves" (the dreamer of the dream and the dream figure in the dream). Upon awakening from sleep, we recognize that what we experienced was in fact a dream, which indicates we know ourselves to be the dreamer, the one who brought the entire dream into existence. This is the one who says, "it was just a dream," with joy, relief, regret, disappointment, or a host of other potential emotions.

We are also aware we dreamed a self, we dreamed others, and we dreamed a world within which we all existed. It would be impossible for any other dream figure to enter or leave my dream world of its own initiative. I would have to dream it in or out of my dream for that to occur. From that point of view, we can grasp that whatever the other figures did in the dream, they did not do through independent volition, as if they were free to make anything up for themselves. We understand *we* made up whatever "they made up" in the dream. This is why dream interpretation can be so useful; it reflects the understanding that the entirety of the dream occurs only in one mind—mine.

There is a fine line between what we call our dreaming and waking states of consciousness. However, both states do share some common characteristics. In both states, there is a single figure I identify as myself. Moreover, much of what occurs in both states is experienced as beyond the control of that figure. In both, there are other figures experienced as separate from myself. Finally, everything occurs within the context of a much greater framework, a world which is separate and independent of the figure known as "me." For that figure, what occurs is experienced as very real, whether awake or asleep.

Perhaps it would help to demonstrate the distinction we are making with an example of someone outside of "me." Imagine we are having a workshop and we are all in a meeting room. During one of the breaks, someone lies down on the floor and falls sleep. What has actually taken place? Someone has merely entered into a different state of consciousness. He has drifted off into a private world, solely of his own making, and he is free to make up and experience anything he wants to.

Who he really is has not changed just because he is asleep and dreaming. This is true regardless of the content of his dream, its intensity or absurdity. He could dream he has died, and he might even scream out loud in the meeting room. Does any of this change the fact that in reality, he is safe, very much alive, and that nothing physical has transpired? Neither he nor the rest of the participants in the workshop have changed. What is taking place?

On one level, we are talking about "pure information," that is, a person is taking a nap. We can observe this. But from the outside, we are not privy to any of the content of his dream. What more do we know if he talks or cries out loud? We are then getting some information about what he seems to be experiencing in the dream, but we do not know why or how. In a weird sort of way, we are straddling two worlds, an asleep world and an awake one. The person asleep on the floor is having an experience in his dream world, but because he is talking in his sleep, he is intersecting us in our awake world. What we have is purely informational because all we are getting is partial content about what the sleeping individual may be experiencing.

Now let's go one step deeper. Imagine that person begins talking in his sleep, and that what he begins talking about is the other people in the workshop. We are now participating—not in the dream itself, for that would be impossible. But we are receiving information from the dream that affects us. To make it even clearer, imagine this man is dreaming about a real event in his history, but one he has kept secret, like an experience of infidelity. What happens then if the spouse is a member of the group? The notion of "purely informational" takes on new meaning.

The point we are making is that although a dream is a dream and not actually happening, what someone experiences in his dreams may have ramifications in his and in others' alternative awake states. These ramifications will have both an internal and an external impact. Internally, I receive information about what is occurring in my own mind. I also become aware that as I act out of that, it will affect others.

Looking at the internal aspect, the natural question is: why am I dreaming me like I am? The answer is simple: it works for me. This is my dream because this is how I *want* it to be. I chose this. I insisted on it, down to the smallest detail. It has brought me everything I ever thought I wanted. I worked very, very hard to get to this place. It did not happen by chance or by accident. I fought and clawed and demanded to be here, and for the most part, I like it. I am willing to change the parts I do not like, one by one, as I am able (and willing) to bring them to consciousness. The parts that do not work often do get changed.

It is that straightforward. However, this also makes me entirely responsible for the parts I do not change. If I knew how to do it any other way, I might—but I do not.

I am who I am, or at least, I am who I *think* I am—and I do think this is who I am, because I *want* it to be me. I *need* it to be me. And each time I encounter a part of me I truly do not like, I disown it entirely and bring someone in my life to hold that for me—someone I judge or criticize or refuse to be in relationship with. This is where external impact occurs.

But if this is true, then where do we go from here? There is a third state we should consider, something called "lucid dreaming." We will define lucid dreaming as a conscious process whereby the dreamer is aware he is dreaming, even to the point of being able to alter what he is dreaming. In the context of our discussion, it means that one is aware of being both the dreamer and the dream figure at the same time. In a sense, the dream is being experienced as real to the dream figure and simultaneously, as "made up" by the dreamer. The recognition of the fundamental unreality of the dream from the lucid state is what accounts for the power of the dreamer to alter the dream for the dream figure.

We maintain that this is an excellent metaphor for what we are calling the "*Awakening Process.*" We can learn to become "lucid dreamers," and as such, begin to change the content of our "dreams," both waking and sleeping. This is hardly a new phenomenon, since the Greek philosopher, Aristotle (4th c. BC), noted that "often when one is asleep, there is something in consciousness which declares that what then presents itself is but a dream."

For example, I could fall asleep and have a horrifying dream of being surrounded by snakes, and when I believe I am the dream figure, my experience might be stark terror. However, if I were in a state of lucid dreaming, I would also be conscious of being the dreamer of the dream. This would mean I would be aware of the dream figure's predicament but would simultaneously be removed from the dream figure's experience of terror. Then, because I am aware of being the dreamer of the dream, I could change what occurs in the dream, and thus change the dream figure's experience. As the dreamer, I can endow the dream figure with magic powers over the snakes, or I can suddenly transform the snakes into butterflies. As the dream figure, I have no control over what is happening, but as the dreamer, I do.

    What does all this mean?

10

Not One Self, but Two

"To the possession of the self the way is inward." Plotinus

We have explored the idea of mind from the vantage point of recognizing there are two aspects of what occurs in our experience when we dream. We have a dreamer who is the creator of the whole dream, and we have a dream figure with which we identify in the dream. We would now like to put the dreamer aside and delve into the single mind of the dream figure. What we will discover is that just as there is a split in consciousness resulting in a dreamer and a dream figure, there is also a split in consciousness within the mind of that single dream figure.

Let's liken the dream figure's experience to that of a human being. Just as that dream figure processes his life in the dream, so we process our lives when we are awake—acting and reacting, choosing and deciding, as if *we* were in control of the outcome.

Again, mirroring the split in consciousness between the dreamer and the dream figure, there is a similar split in *Consciousness* in each human being, which means we are of a dual nature. In this book, we have identified the two aspects of this dual nature as Bear and Reindeer.

With no thought at all, we take for granted that we are one self. After all, we occupy a single body, with one brain, living in one place in space and time. But the *Truth* of experience reveals we have a dual nature, which produces two different states of being, and thereby results in two distinct selves. The lack of recognition of our dual nature has been one of the greatest impediments in all attempts to understand human experience, as well as the evolution of human *Consciousness*.

It is not difficult to recognize that all human beings have varying degrees of identification with and/or devotion to each one of these natures within us—that is, to the Bear or to the Reindeer. Those varying degrees of our identifications with the Bear or the Reindeer are significant in that they reflect the differences in the degree to which we are "en-darkened" or enlightened, asleep or awake. Furthermore, it is those identifications which drive what we believe, think, and do.

These ideas lead us onward and inward, but the mere acceptance of the notion of our dual nature, or even the willingness to entertain the possibility of two selves, is not enough. The next hurdle is to challenge the belief these two selves could ever be integrated. They cannot, and as we will explain, the deeper understanding of this fact becomes a crucial step in this process.

Earlier, we suggested any attempt to blend two different radio stations playing different music programs would not only be impossible, but absurd. Likewise, the belief that our two selves can—or *need* to—be integrated, has resulted in a huge misunderstanding of *Consciousness*—what it is, how it works, and how this evolution of *Consciousness* impacts our lives. A goal of integrating the two selves not only totally misses the point, but sets people off in the wrong direction, down a path which has no end, simply because it is impossible. Our two selves cannot be integrated because they rest on two irreconcilable thought systems.

One of the most difficult ideas we are trying to convey is that each of us possesses two selves who are living in *Parallel Universes simultaneously*. Moreover, they have no intersection. This means at any given moment in time, both selves are processing what occurs in this world, but they are doing so through thought systems that have no overlap or connection whatsoever.

That we are two very distinct selves slips by unnoticed in our ongoing experience, because we move back and forth between these two selves so rapidly. Even if one were aware of when this happens, she might not know or understand *how* it is happening. In essence then, we are not a single self, housed in one body, and run by one mind. We are two selves housed in one body and run by one *Mind*.

Remember we spoke of two strangers standing side by side watching the same event. They may be seeing the same thing with their physical eyes, but it is highly unlikely that they will be having an identical experience of the event. The idea that those two individuals would have vastly different experiences is much more acceptable, even reconcilable, in our minds, than the idea that the same thing might be true in the context of an individual psyche. But who hasn't had the experience of seeing a person or an event one way at one moment in time, and very differently at another?

There are two possible explanations for what takes place when that happens. The first is that we simply "*changed our mind about*" something. We got new information, we had time to think more about it, or we talked to someone else about it, and as a result, we "*changed our mind about*" what we were thinking. The other possibility is that we *Changed Minds,* which is more akin to the two people having very different experiences of a shared event. **Changing Minds** *is* connected to the two different selves and points directly to the two universes.

When something occurs in our lives that is unexpected or contrary to what we anticipated, we have two options available to us for reaction. The first is to move into crisis, because what has happened is not how we thought it would happen. At some level, the unexpected event is threatening, and crisis ensues. We would have felt "safe" if what happened had occurred as we thought it would.

In contrast to that, **Changing Minds** means I make room for exactly how it did happen, and in so doing, take on the threat it presented to my mind, and try to see it for what it really is. I make the effort to integrate the unexpected without shattering the stable world I thought I knew and lived in.

Imagine that I have a dear friend whom I believed would stand beside me forever—no matter what. I share with her an intensely personal experience which I would never believe she could judge me for. I could not be more surprised then, when this friend rejects me and turns away from me. Painfully, there is no part of my mind that can comprehend this. I cannot "*change my mind about*" it enough to make it fit.

Therefore, my real task is to *Change Minds*, which means that instead of focusing on the threat imposed on me in my mind, I expand my *Consciousness* to include *her* mind, too. In this larger space, other questions can arise, like "what is s*he* dealing with?" "How did the personal experience I shared threaten her?" "Why does she feel like rejecting me makes her feel safer?"

Changing my mind about something occurs within a single state of *Consciousness*, the same universe. In stark contrast, when I C*hange Minds*, I am changing universes, changing identifications, occupying a completely different self. I am not attempting to see something differently through the eyes of the same self, I am looking through the eyes of a different self, who literally *sees* it differently. It does not stem from an effort to change what I am thinking or feeling in the same mind. That merely brings about the illusion of change," and in so doing, postpones real change. **C*hanging Minds*** occurs because there has been a shift in *Consciousness*, accessing a different way of experiencing it altogether.

The illusion of change mentioned above is profoundly important. This is what keeps us confused—and mistakenly satisfied. We settle for our ideas of better or more spiritual or more evolved, when no meaningful change has in fact occurred. My so-called *change of mind* is an attempt to see something differently within the same universe, because I want to see myself in a better light. I have the illusion of "feeling better," but I have merely put off genuine transformation. Something only truly happens when we C*hange Minds*. This is where we experience a genuine alternative. The obvious question then is: "*Who* is having that experience?"

11

The Witness and the Observer

"The greatest obstacle to discovery is not ignorance - it is the illusion of knowledge." Daniel J. Boorstin

There is a state of *Consciousness* in my waking state of mind comparable to that of lucid dreaming. In lucid dreaming, there is a *Consciousness* that includes the simultaneous experience of the dreamer and the dream figure. In my waking state of mind, there can also be the simultaneous experience of what is occurring with the "me" in my mind that is, as a figure in my own "waking dream," as well as a perspective that includes the awareness of a more expansive "me" that *knows* I am making up my experience.

In the normal course of our experience, I believe there is a "me" who unwittingly experiences the various events occurring in "my" life as I move through space and time. But as I gain more and more consciousness of what is actually going on, I become increasingly aware that "my" experience is being generated by what I am making up about the events I encounter. In a sense, then, I begin to experience my life as if it is being dreamed. Said another way, I become aware that one aspect of "me" is having a normal human experience, and simultaneously, another aspect of "me" knows that "I" am generating this whole thing.

One way to explain this phenomenon is to create a distinction between these two different positions in the mind: one we will call a *Witness* and the other an *Observer*. There is a dramatic difference in experience between these two, and this is in no way based on what anyone does.

In our normal dreaming experience, there are three basic scenarios that describe how we remember our dreams. One is that we have a dream at night, awaken during the dream, and realize we are dreaming. Another is that upon waking, we remember a particular dream or a portion of a dream that we had some time while we were sleeping. A third scenario is that upon waking, we do not immediately recall having had a particular dream, but something happens during the day that triggers our remembering the dream. This remembering is the most limited though, representing only a recollection of disparate parts of the dream. In our effort to remember the dream, there is usually no consciousness of the fact that the dream was fully orchestrated within the mind of the dreamer, the person who was asleep.

We propose there is an Observer and a Witness in both our waking and sleeping states of *Consciousness*. The Observer in the context of the dream state is in the mind of the dream figure. The Observer in the context of our waking state is in the mind of a normal human being going about his life. In both cases, this Observer processes events as they occur and has reactions to what is going on. He seems to be involved in what happens. He may note he is happy or angry, peaceful or upset, acting calmly or irrationally, etc., but all he can do is observe. He has no power to do anything about what he observes. He cannot intervene or change anything—which makes him a kind of victim of events over which he has no control.

In contrast to the Observer, the Witness occupies a very different position in the *Mind*—a much higher state of *Consciousness*. His experience is much like that of the lucid dreamer. The lucid dreamer is outside of the dream, and the Witness is outside of the events occurring in his waking experience. Much like the lucid dreamer who recognizes that the dream is being orchestrated from the mind of the person asleep, the Witness recognizes that his life experience is likewise orchestrated by the mind of the individual living his life. Because the Witness is not wholly identified with that individual, he is not bound by what is occurring, and therefore, has the power to affect what is happening—in fact, to change everything.

In the heightened state of awareness of the Witness, there is a sense of detachment which is often marked by a sense of expansiveness or spaciousness. This transcendent feeling is something almost everyone has experienced at some time— perhaps listening to a beautiful piece of music or watching a glorious sunset. Far too often, though, such an experience is readily dismissed as exceptional, and mistakenly associated with the specifics of what has just occurred. Doing so obscures what has actually happened. It also leads us on a wild goose chase to recapture the extraordinary feelings by recreating the specific experience rather than the change in *Consciousness* the experience provoked.

As the Witness, we do not create what is witnessed. Nor do we create the spaciousness that may accompany this state of

Mind. Rather, this spaciousness is a natural consequence of letting go of our attachment to being a tiny figure in an enormous waking dream. Letting go frees us to access a space that already always is. This space, this shift of *Consciousness* is an ever-present possibility. What has really happened is we *Changed Minds.* Perhaps unknowingly, and despite varying degrees of intensity, the state change itself is unmistakable.

Our ever-changing experience of this phenomenon is caused by our shifting back and forth between minds, between the positions in our minds of Witness and Observer. We will continue to remember and forget. We will continue to find ourselves in the powerless state of observation, and then find ourselves in the power and spaciousness of the Witness. Every time we bring awareness to these shifts, in either direction, from Observer to Witness or vice versa, we evolve. We will find increasing clarity about what is happening, and why. And with this increasing awareness, we resurrect our power to choose which position we want to occupy.

12

Waking from the Dream

"Your vision will become clear only when you look into your heart. Who looks outside, dreams. Who looks inside, awakens." Carl Gustav Jung

To take a huge leap forward, what would open up for us if we entertained the possibility that our waking experience is fundamentally no different than our dreaming experience? Teasing out this possibility is the task at hand. This initially leads us to the question: "What is the *Mind?*"

Let us acknowledge at the outset that without a deep appreciation of what is being said here, an initial attempt to equate the experience of an awake self with a dream figure may appear absurd. For example, my dreaming one of my children died is obviously very different than the actual death of my child in this world. This is *not* where we are directing you. What we are asking you to do is entertain some new ways of thinking, some new possibilities, and see where they lead you.

We are pointing to the *Mind*. By using the context of a dream, it is possible to elaborate the two levels of *Mind*: the mind of the dreamer, and the more restricted mind of the individual dream figure. The individual mind of the dream figure is just a tiny perspective on all that is occurring in the dream. In contrast, the mind of the dreamer is infinitely more expansive. In fact, it is the context in which everything is occurring, and it contains all of the individual dream figures' perspectives.

The difference between the two would be like the difference in perspective between someone standing six inches from a wall 10-feet high and 20 feet wide, and someone standing six feet back from it. The person standing six inches from the wall believes he is seeing the entire wall—and it *is* the "entire wall" for him from that limited perspective. The problem is that it is clearly not the entire wall. From six feet back, the view of the wall is different and may include a much larger perspective, but it is still not the "entire wall." And of course, the view of the "entire wall" changes yet again for someone standing fifteen feet back, thirty feet back, etc.

Now consider that a similar thing might be occurring in our waking experience. The individual we call ourselves is merely a tiny perspective on something much grander. Each expanded perspective leads to a greater appreciation of the whole of what is going on, and ultimately leads to the possibility that we are not a single self located in one specific point in space in time, rather we share a *Consciousness* that would be the equivalent of the mind of the dreamer.

What is the significance of accessing this *Conscious Mind?* It would shatter what we have believed to be the reality of what we experience through the limits of our singular self, and the limited perspective of someone standing only six inches from the wall. It would give us access to a more expansive reality that can only be seen and known from a position much further back.

In what we normally call the "real" world, that is, in our normal state of consciousness, what we are aware of is the single dream figure I call "me," and then a huge world with lots of people running around in it who appear to be independent of "me." Part of the challenge is figuring out what to do with that world "out there," which certainly appears to be—and *is* experienced as—separate from me, independent of me, and viewed as definitely *not* of my making. Nothing in my experience would support anything suggesting there is not something "out there," outside of me. I am not responsible for you. I am not responsible for what you do. I am not responsible for the events that take place on this planet, most of which I am not even aware.

Part of what we need to understand is the application of the idea of separation here. Simply expressed, the separation here is manifested as "me" and "not me." My experience here dictates there is an object I call "me" and an entire universe outside of that "me," basically, what I perceive as my "not me." All that exists, then, is "me" and "not me." "Me" is an object I hold as myself (my bodily, psychological self), and then, of course, everything that is not part of that experience of "me" is "not me." It is the entire world in which my "me" exists.

Now let's put this in the context of the *Mind,* going back to what we explored about the dream state. The entire dream is happening within the mind of the dreamer, the individual asleep and lying in the bed. It is *not* happening within the mind of the one small dream figure I identify as "me" in the dream. Remember, the dream figure is only one small aspect of the entire mind of the dreamer. That dream figure is merely the "me" and does not include any of the "not me." The dream figure experiences only itself within the context of the entire universe in which it exists.

"Me" is an object in my mind, as is my "not me." So what happens in the mind in my experience is that the object I call "me" intersects, bumps into, interfaces with another object in my "not me" world. The object "me," opens my eyes and sees the "not me" object, you. An experience occurs. My "me" has the experience (a thought or a feeling or a reaction) regarding my relationship to my "not me," you. It could be said that "I" am just one perspective on experiencing some kind of relationship between two objects in my mind. To be clear: we are not saying the mind in which the experience occurs is "me." The mind in which the experience occurs includes both "me" *and* "not me" (you). "I" is just a point of reference in that process.

Here's where this is all leading. The Reindeer/ego mind is impersonal; it is pre-programmed. It is the Reindeer's infinite and self-serving perspective on what happens when one object in the universe intersects another seemingly separate object in the universe. This is how experience occurs. It does feel personal because it is about *my* "me" and *my* thoughts about everything that is "not me." If we look more deeply, however, we can begin to see that what we are really talking about is our conditioning. Oddly enough, it means that to some degree, my experience is not even "mine." It is what I have learned through my family, my culture, my education, my history.

The *Mind*, then, is merely a field of possibilities. It is the matrix in which all specific actions and all potential responses to all actions are contained. There are, of course, infinite possible actions and therefore, infinite sets of responses that could arise.

We become a Witness to each of those specific actions as they arise and simultaneously, we become a Witness to the arising of all possible responses. The Witness is a position in the *Mind* that is not attached to the experience, and is therefore free to merely be with what is exposed. The key is that all of it is completely impersonal. It is all merely *Mind* made manifest. What an amazing opportunity to be Witness to the *Mind!*

As the Reindeer mind is relinquished, each of us becomes a Witness to an *Awakening*. We are Witnesses to mind awakening to what is *True*. What does this mean for me personally? Freedom. In dreaming, we are free to dream anything we want, with absolutely no limitations. Then we awaken and remember what we dreamt is not true. We are pressing you to see your waking experience in the same light. You are not limited by the tiny figure you call your "self." Nor are you bound by the laws of a singular Reindeer universe. You can awaken to the idea that you are merely dreaming, that your Reindeer's choices are *not* true. To accomplish this, we next explore the distinctions between *Form and Content*.

13

Form and Content

"The lunar flights give you a correct perception of our existence. You look back at Earth from the moon, and you can put your thumb up to the window and hide the Earth behind your thumb. Everything you've ever known is behind your thumb, and that blue-and-white ball is orbiting a rather normal star, tucked away on the outer edge of a galaxy." James Arthur "Jim" Lovell

Most of us have little to no awareness—or even curiosity—of how experience occurs. This is as true in the pettiness of our everyday lives as it is on a much grander scale of life and death. We spend most of our lives in an unconscious sea of assumptions and interpretations—and most often, we are unthinkingly "satisfied" that this is just "how it is," or we settle for what we have, believing "this is as good as it gets." We do not stop to think or seek to recognize that most of how and why we experience what we do is based on what has gone before, that is, specifically what has been passed on to us from others—

parents, grandparents, friends, neighbors, cultures, countries, etc. In a sense, then, we are like generational carrier pigeons, passing on from generation to generation the various concepts, beliefs, and even world views we have received and unquestioningly accept as true.

Think about it. Where did your ideas about religion or politics come from? Obviously, each of us has free will, and we can choose to *change our minds about* things, to differ from what our parents and others think, but on the whole, we move forward along the same well-worn paths our ancestors trod. Please note this is not a condemnation, but rather an observation, and a call to awaken to the fact that this is what is going on. Why do you believe what you believe? What is the effect of your beliefs? This leads us into the realm of experience.

Fundamentally, experience is born when one of our senses interacts with the external world. Take, for instance, the sense of sight. We think we "see" the beauty of a sunrise, or the devastation of a tornado. This is not what we "see" at all. What we call "seeing" is merely our eyes reporting data to us, but this is far from a simple process. It goes something like this: the retinas in our eyes receive light waves that set off complex chemical reactions that create electrical impulses in the optic nerves. Those electrical impulses then transmit information to our brains, which piece the data together to form what we "see." However, the data reported is upside-down, and the brain "rights" it through a process called perceptual adaptation. In essence, the eyes report only the *Form* of things in our external world, like size and shape and color. When we say we "saw" a beautiful sunrise, what we are really saying is that our eyes reported to our brains this vast array of shapes and colors and texture and light. To speak of the sunrise as "beautiful" is *Content*, and can only be an interpretation of that data.

So, there are actually two levels of experiencing, almost as if there are two levels of "seeing." One level is *Form*, that of my senses reporting the effect of light waves to my brain, which is a physiological process that remains totally unconscious to me. A separate level is *Content*, that is, what I am making up about what those light waves report, the interpretation or the meaning I am giving them. Likewise unconscious to us, this constitutes my experience of life.

The question we would raise then is this: just as in the physical aspect of sight, where the images are upside down and are "righted" by the brain, is it possible the interpretations that we are giving the data are likewise upside down as well and need to be "righted"?

At the physiological level, the brain is neutral and does nothing more than record data, and significantly, in a consistent way. The brain makes absolutely no choices about which data to capture. It "sees" everything. But then the mind takes over and tries to "right" the images in an attempt to achieve a similar consistency. But it can only do so by manipulating the evidence to compensate for small differences that are inherently part of what we think we see. In this way, our experience remains consistent and we find what we *expect* to "see."

It is critical to make this important distinction between **Form and Content**. It should be clear by now that *Form* is about what my eyes report. It is about what is physically happening in my world. *Content* is about what I make up about that, the meaning I ascribe to it. The simple point is that we do not realize or understand that our physical eyes are not "seeing" what we are *experiencing*. What we are experiencing is based only on the meaning we are giving to what we see.

One of the keys to understanding *Consciousness* is perspective. If our planet, Earth, is viewed from far out in space, it looks like a little blue dot. If our planet is viewed from an orbiting satellite, it begins to take on different shapes and colors, so that land masses and water can be detected. If we look at Earth from a commercial jet flying at 32,000 feet, we can see distinct rivers, mountains, cities. As the jet descends, we can begin to make out moving cars on freeways, specific landmarks, even billboards. At each increasing level of proximity, our perspective changes, and more and more detail comes into view.

So it is with *Consciousness*. From a totally unconscious perspective, we might believe that we are just individually processing what is "true" out there in the world. This is where many of us live—unthinking, unquestioning, unchanging. From a more conscious perspective, we become increasingly aware that we are not seeing what is "true" out there, but only what is "true" from an individual's perspective—*my* interpretations, *my* meanings, *my* reality.

Another way of saying this is that as we process all the information reported to us, what we are in fact "seeing" is our beliefs, projected onto the forms "out there." *What* I think about what is occurring and how I feel about what is occurring, is what I erroneously call "seeing"—and this is not only *in* my world, it *is* my world. I become aware of what I believe only by examining my interpretations of what is happening. Meaning is not "out there" in the world, independent of my mind. Meaning is the *Content* in my mind. This accounts for why people "see" things so differently: they have different beliefs about what they are seeing.

This in itself is not a novel idea. Freud coined the term "projection" to account for this phenomenon. We are always in the act of projecting. One element of the evolution of

Consciousness is learning to *be with* our projections. Our projections reveal our minds to us. Once we realize that our projections are not reality, choice is introduced into the system. This is so because if meaning and truth were "out there," independent of us, we would be helpless victims of our world and slaves of our unconscious projections.

If meaning is not a projection, what each of us is encountering is merely his beliefs about his own "out there." However, changing what we *believe* about what is "out there" gives us choice, and choice raised to awareness allows us to recognize that we do have a say about our lives and our experiences. With the awareness of choice, we are able to question, challenge, and refine what we think and what we believe. But even so, this is merely *changing our minds about* something. The real impact comes only when we *Change Minds.*

14

Form and Content: Purpose

"Men are disturbed not by things, but by the view which they take of them." Epictetus

    The radical shift in *Consciousness* we propose begins with the understanding that at all times, there are, as we have previously stated, two *Parallel Universes* that exist simultaneously. It is almost as if you drew a line beginning at your nose that extends forward into infinity. On the right side, there is the Bear universe, and on the left side, there is the Reindeer universe. Your experience at any given time depends on which universe you choose to "see" from in that moment. For this single choice determines your entire experience.
    Far-reaching change starts with a willingness to challenge the basic suppositions you unconsciously hold—those that guide your life. Before we get into any specifics about these suppositions, let us give you an example of how these work, and

the consequences of the erroneous conclusions we draw from them.

Imagine you observe a 13-year-old boy bullying his fellow classmates. You become uncomfortable with his behavior, and as his bullying escalates, so do your reactions. The discomfort becomes irritation, which then becomes anger, and finally, you feel compelled to intervene. Why? Because at the root of your thinking is a fundamental belief that "correct behavior" includes respect and at the very least, civility, and any incidence of bullying is simply wrong. So what do you think of the bully? In an instant, he becomes your "enemy," something to be overcome, stopped, even punished. Do not overlook the fact that you have also "learned" that misdeeds *require* punishment.

But suppose you suddenly learn this bully is an orphan, whose single, drug-addicted mother abandoned him at a fire station? And then you learn he was raised in an orphanage where there was a severe staff shortage, and for several days, no one even noticed this baby had not eaten or had his diapers changed. And then imagine you learn he was put into foster care where his foster mother was severely depressed, and his alcoholic foster father beat him every night when he came home from the bar.

Now how do you feel about the bully?

This deeper understanding does not mean you do not intervene to stop the bullying. It does mean, however, that you are likely do so from a different place in your *Mind*. In fact—and this is critically important—it is a different *Mind* altogether. Where before there was only blame and judgment, now there is compassion and sympathy. The goal of your intervention, then, is no longer punishment, but peace—and perhaps something more for the bully. Kindness? Support? Help?

These are the same two minds you use when you overlook

something your best friend does but criticize your spouse for the identical behavior. How can that be? This is the paradox of processing the same information through two different minds.

Changing Minds is a choice that indicates you have moved to a different place to experience whatever you are experiencing. The event itself may not change at all, but when you C*hange Minds*, everything is processed differently. You do not *change your mind about* what someone else did, you change the lens through which you process it. If you look through a red lens, the whole world is red, and all you can do is try to make distinctions between "this red" and "that red," "lighter red" and "darker red." But if you take off the red lens and put on blue lens, there is no red at all—anywhere—to be processed. You will never see anything blue in your red world, nor anything red in your blue world.

Value defines what each world is based on, what can be accomplished in *Form* versus what is *True*. A good illustration of this would be the parable of the "Rich Young Ruler" in the *Bible (*Matthew 19:16-22, NIV*)*. The Rich Young Ruler comes to Jesus and asks: "What must I do to be saved?" Jesus tells him to follow the Commandments, and this young man replies he has done so from his youth. Then Jesus tells him: "Go, sell what you have and give to the poor, and you will have treasure in heaven; and come, follow Me."

But the young man turns and leaves, full of sorrow, because he is very wealthy. The Rich Young Ruler had done everything right in *Form*, and that mind of *Form* is the place from which he asked Jesus the question. This is also why he could not truly hear Jesus' answer. From the wrong place of listening (the Reindeer mind), he thought Jesus was talking about *Form*, telling him to give up everything he owned. This is where his value was. But Jesus was not talking about *Form*, he was focusing entirely on *Content*. His answer had nothing to do with *Form*. Jesus told the young man to give up, not his worldly possessions, but rather everything that stood in the way of his genuine relationship with Jesus.

While we are in the *Bible*, let's look at another example of the difference between *Form and Content*. In the story of the "widow's mite" (Mark 12:41-44, NIV), Jesus is near the place where people make their offerings, and he sees many rich people throwing in large amounts of money. Then he observes a widow, who puts in two small copper coins, worth only a few cents. And he says: "Truly I tell you, this poor widow has put more into the treasury than all the others. They all gave out of their wealth; but she, giving out of her poverty, put in everything—all she had to live on." From *Form*, we might ask how her little offering could be more valuable than all the other large amounts put together? After all, enormous good could be done with a large sum of money. The difference is the mind from which the offering was made. From *Form*, the quantity is what mattered; from *Content*, it was the gift that counted, and the heart that gave that small gift of two copper coins gave everything.

The point being made here is that we mistakenly give great credence to *Form*. We automatically assume *Form* dictates meaning and significance. But in doing so, we miss the point altogether. *Form* could be an action that has nothing whatsoever to do with what is actually taking place. It is an error in the way we process that requires an extraordinary willingness to challenge what we think is taking place, and an even greater commitment to overcome the strength of our belief in that error in our thinking.

15

Form and Content: Practice

"I think the greatest illusion we have is that denial protects us. It's actually the biggest distortion and lie. In fact, staying asleep is what's killing us." Eve Ensler

We want to drive home the difference between **Form and Content**, and to address the dilemma we face every time we resist **Changing Minds**. Let's be clear: as long as we are in these physical bodies on this physical plane, we must honor *Form*, but we do not have to be at its mercy! We often get stuck in *Form* because it looks like *Form* carries meaning. In a sense, our life experiences have trained us to believe this is so. But if that is true, then there is no *Innocence* anywhere. This is the very basis of the Reindeer mind.

Form is neutral—although it is certainly not meaningless to us in our experience. *Form* absolutely carries the evidence of what is happening in our world. With every incident (word, gesture, event, etc.) that occurs, we can believe the meaning *Form* conveys, or we can look deeper for the meaning *Content* makes possible.

Content can be known, but it cannot be substantiated—for it simply does not "fit" in the Reindeer universe. This creates a dilemma: do we go with the *Content* that cannot be backed up in this world or do we fall back to the Reindeer mind and convince ourselves of something that is not *True*? To do that, we must "tamper with the evidence"—justify and rationalize our thoughts so they "fit" in with everything else we believe.

Take the experience of rape, for example. The world says such an event should be traumatic for every rape victim, right? So how can we understand the young woman who forgives her attacker and moves on with her life, at peace with herself and the world? If indeed we believe rape should be traumatic, then forgiveness does not make sense. This means we have to manipulate the evidence of this young woman's forgiveness by telling ourselves: "she had a different upbringing," or "she has greater faith in God," or "she has a better support system to cope with this"—anything that allows our personal belief system to remain intact.

It is the nature of mind to think *Form* is the problem, which would mean the solution must be in *Form*, too. This is often where we first look. The Reindeer mind is bound to *Form*, by experience, by history, by culture. We do look for answers in *Form*, but we will never find them there. It would be like putting on red glasses hoping to see blue. So how do we resolve this paradox? How do we escape?

We discover that our experience is always being directed by our thought system, either Reindeer or Bear. But there are limits to the thought system of *Form*, like holding your breath under water because you want to be a fish. It is simply not possible. Each thought system precludes the other, and neither depends on the other: this one here does not *cause* that one. In the Reindeer's thought system, we cling to a belief that this world is real, that we are victims, and most often, powerless. We accept our victim status, we settle into denial, or we "tamper with the evidence"—whatever it takes to keep the Reindeer mind alive and in control.

In the Bear's thought system, we honor the insanity and the brutality at the level of *Form*, for *Form* must be acknowledged, but we do not run our thinking through *Form* to determine our experience. We move to *Content*, that is, we *Change Minds*, to determine that. We stay in contact with whatever the experience is, with whatever "they" are doing, but we remain completely in charge of what it all *means*.

Form may not carry meaning, but it does expose what we are thinking. What do we say when someone explains a difficult concept and we finally grasp it? "Oh, I *see*...." This is obviously not with our eyes! We can see what is happening in *Form*, or we can truly "*see*." "I see" equals understanding, and we are saying that understanding is glimpsing the *Truth*. Nothing is stabilized in perception, it is always associated with some way we are processing it. We can "see" what our mind is telling us is true, or we can begin to "see" there is something else.

We cannot "see" *Innocence* or *Love* in *Form*. We can see expressions of these, but not in the *Form* itself. The French writer and aviation pioneer, Antoine de St. Exupéry said it like this: "It is only with the heart that one can see rightly. What is essential is invisible to the eye."

Let us conclude the discussion of *Form and Content* with one last example from the *Bible*, the story of Jesus on the Cross. Jesus' jailers had mercilessly beaten him, pressed a crown of thorns on his head, and nailed him to a cross. Still, he prayed:

"Father, forgive them, for they do not know what they are doing" (Luke 23:34, NIV). The words: "...they do not know what they are doing" was not a rationalization or a justification for his jailers' actions. His forgiveness was not about *Form*. Indeed, in *Form*, his prayer changed nothing. In *Form*, they still crucified him. But in *Content*, his prayer changed everything, because it was a recognition of the *Truth* that nothing they or anyone else did excluded them from *God's Love*. In *Content*, he died "in relationship" with his persecutors—by choice, and from the Bear mind.

Changing Minds is not *changing your mind about* anything. You may encounter resistance in the thought: "But this does not make sense!" And you will be right: it does not make sense in this world. You have to *look* somewhere else to *see* something else. We are definitely not talking about "positive thinking" or about manipulating this reality. We are talking about thoughts—and thoughts are in the mind. In the end, our experience is not determined by what is happening, but only by our thoughts about what is happening.

With this book, we want to create an ever more conscious perspective, helping you "see "beyond what seems to be true "out there," and far beyond what each of us is making up about it. Such a new perspective leads us much more deeply into the *Mind*, the source of why and how we experience life as we do. Only there is it possible to "*Change Minds.*"

16

Not "It" but not "Not It"

"What can we gain by sailing to the moon if we are not able to cross the abyss that separates us from ourselves? This is the most important of all voyages of discovery, and without it, all the rest are not only useless, but disastrous." Thomas Merton

My experience is very important. But its importance is not defined by the criterion of either accuracy or truth. That would totally miss the point. What makes my experience important is that it is *my* experience. We need to delve more deeply into this. We would challenge the often-used statement, "It is what it is," for this does not take into account what makes it "what it is."

The implied connotation in the statement, "It is what it is," is that we should just "deal with it," address what is occurring in our lives. There is a huge problem with this idea. How many times have we thought we understood "what it is" means, only to discover that we were wrong about "it?" The paradoxical and whimsical title of this chapter helps us understand this.

The best way to deepen our understanding of the "Not 'It,' but not 'Not It'" paradox would be to return to our earlier discussion of what happens when we dream at night. Most people are familiar with the psychological technique of dream interpretation. According to this process, what happens in a dream is considered to be highly symbolic, and therefore significant. The assumption is that what an individual dreams at night is rich with meaning, because it taps into the subconscious world of the individual. It is not as if the dream is simply coming out of nowhere.

When a person falls asleep and dreams, some part of his mind is creating the dream, and within the context of the dream, whatever happens in the dream is real for that individual; it is "what it is" for that individual at that moment. Events occur, people come and go, emotions are felt. This is absolutely what is true on one level. There is another level, however, that transpires simultaneously, and this is what dream interpretation points to. The dream is occurring in the mind of the dreamer, and it is very real for the dreamer, but it is also simultaneously not real, because it is not occurring in actual space and time.

Here is a simple example of dreaming and how dream interpretation works. Imagine a man who reports that he dreamed he was sitting on a beach somewhere, listening to the waves crash against the shore, feeling the wind blow through his hair, and basking in the warmth of the sun, very much at peace. Then, suddenly and most unexpectedly, a blue stork walks up to him. In his dream state, this was his experience. This is what occurred for him, is "what it is," but it did not occur in reality, in his physical, awake reality.

Further imagine that later the same day, the man's wife calls and reports she is pregnant, and the doctor has told her the baby is a boy. Dream interpretation reveals that the unreal, ridiculous dream of a blue stork walking up to the man on a beach was highly symbolic. The stork is obviously a symbol of a baby on the way, and the fact that the stork was blue indicated that the baby was a boy. We are not talking about prophecy, but rather symbolism.

How might we further use the idea of dream interpretation? What if we approached our waking state using the same lines of thinking? What if we thought of our everyday experience as our "waking dreams?" What if our "waking dreams" are no different than our "sleeping dreams," if what occurs to us in our daily lives is simultaneously occurring on two levels, just as it is in dreaming? On one level, what happens, happens. It "is what it is." On another level though, what if, just as when we dream, it is also purely symbolic?

We propose that our lives are paradoxically not "It," but at the same time, not "Not It." If our lives are "waking dreams," then just as with our sleeping dreams, they are not real, and cannot be "It." But they are "what is" at some level, so they are also not insignificant, which makes them not "Not It." They are real to us and carry very important meaning about what is going on in our minds. Freud said that "dreams are the royal road to the unconscious workings of the mind." Another great teacher took this idea even further to say that "Our *lives* are the royal road to the unconscious workings of the mind."

It is essential we remember that what occurs in our lives does not carry inherent meaning. Our experience of what occurs is shaped by our minds, which is then projected out onto what occurs. One of the reasons there is so much conflict in the world is because nothing is simply "true" in and of itself. It is not just "what it is." It is shaped by personal and collective history, culture, age, race, gender, etc. All of us lead our lives, basing what we do on our beliefs about what is "true." But how dependable is that? What is "true" constantly changes.

Think how much almost everything we thought was "true" has changed over just the brief years of our lifetime, with subjects as commonplace as medicine or nutrition. Imagine, then, the gulf between now and 100 years ago! Then consider what might be "true" in the future. Perhaps you will remember the physician called "Bones" on the original Star Trek series. Centuries ahead of us, he once watched a video on surgery in the 21st century and proclaimed it to be "barbaric." What we hold as "true" now is only "true" *now* and promises to change soon.

As one last pointer to what we are saying, let's reprise the idea of lucid dreaming discussed in a previous chapter. We defined lucid dreaming as a state of consciousness in which one simultaneously has the experience of being both the dreamer in a bed dreaming, and a dream figure in the dream being dreamt. The lucid dreamer has the awareness that because it is a dream, what is occurring in the dream is not "It." But he also knows that as a dream figure in the dream, what is occurring for him is a very "real" experience, so it is certainly not "Not It."

"Not 'It,' but not 'Not It,'" is the dividing line between two levels of existence. "It" refers to what I am experiencing. "Not It" refers to the fact that what I am experiencing is not "true." The "not 'Not It'" refers to the fact that what I am experiencing *is* important—to me. It is vital that we do not deny what we are experiencing on the grounds that it is not "It." We must look at our experience precisely *because* it is also not "Not It." We look because it gives us access to our minds, to what leads us to believe and think about what is "true." Our goal is to go beyond our "It," our "Not It," and our "not 'Not It'" to an experience of something more transcendent, something beyond what each of us merely believes.

In conclusion, there is a Zen parable that reminds us that we may use a boat to cross a river, but once across, we do not want to drag the boat with us. We leave it behind. It has served its purpose. The boat was "It" when it needed to be, but it is not "It" anymore.

17

Cause & Effect

"Because our entire universe is made up of consciousness, we never really experience the universe directly we just experience our consciousness of the universe, our perception of it, so right, our only universe is perception." Alan Moore

We live within the illusion that life occurs in "billiard ball fashion." Capturing how billiard balls operate in relationship to each other on a pool table reflects how we think our world happens, that is, in a linear, **Cause and Effect** fashion where one action provokes a second, which produces a third, and so on. A pool cue strikes a cue ball, which strikes a colored ball, which, with skill, then rolls into a pool table pocket.

In this sequence of events, moving the cue stick becomes cause, and the cue ball being struck becomes an effect. Then the cue ball striking another ball becomes cause, and the colored ball being struck becomes an effect. At the end of the day—or the game, as it were—we understand what happens as a linear progression of "this happened first, which caused that to happen, in sequence," and so on.

Within such a line of thinking, cause and effect are separate, but always in relationship to one another. One independent event occurs, which leads to a series of dependent events. The cue ball would not have moved unless struck by the pool cue, and the colored ball would not have changed position unless struck by the cue ball. It is linear and relational. Understanding this reality as it occurs on a pool table is absolutely essential because it does not deny that this is how the universe functions on one level: the most common level of human experience, our physical existence. However, the *Cause and Effect* that takes place on this physical plane is not the *Cause and Effect* that occurs in the *Mind* in the *Parallel Universes* we are introducing.

What we rather want to focus on and further explore is the notion of *Cause and Effect* as it operates in the *Mind*, in the realm of *Consciousness*. We cannot overemphasize that this bears no resemblance to how *Cause and Effect* operates at the level of our physicality. The contrast is quite startling, for in our 3-D world, cause and effect are independent, while in the *Mind*, *Cause and Effect* are not independent of each other at all. In that realm, *Cause and Effect* are simultaneous, they are one.

Take a moment to think of a simple coin with two sides. The heads and tails on the two sides of this coin in no way cause each other. In fact, the coin itself only exists as a simultaneous relationship between heads and tails. We postulate that this same phenomenon of simultaneous relationship exists with respect to the idea of *experience* in the *Mind*.

Let us begin with the pure phenomenon of perception. There is the experience of *Cause and Effect* in the "billiard ball universe," and our personal ongoing experience seems to occur in much the same way. It looks like an event that occurs "out there" causes an experience in my mind, my internal world, which in turn causes some reaction in the physical world. But what if the occurrence of something "out there," and what seems like my resultant "internal experience" of it were, like the two sides of a coin, inseparable—absolutely and always simultaneous?

We all fall prey to believing that what happens "out there" as an event is what is causing a reaction in our mind. With this book, we are trying to raise awareness of the fact that what actually happens is we discover that we are mere witnesses to our beliefs about what any particular "that" means in relationship to a "this," in other words, our interpretation of "that." For that relationship *is* already, even *always*, in place; it is set.

Think about it. It takes not one jot of time, or even the slightest effort to know what any "that" means when it happens. "That" already has an association, a meaning, an interpretation, and all we ever do is access the part of our mind where that particular event triggers "this" meaning in my mind—where we think we know what it means. We all know what winning the lottery or receiving the birthday present we asked for or hearing a child giggle means. We assume we know because of our relationship to it. In our minds, "this" *does* mean "that," and we are caught by surprise if all of a sudden, it ever seems to mean something else. This is all further complicated by the fact that "this" and "that" can and most likely will mean something entirely different to your sibling and your best friend and a total stranger.

To reiterate, in my everyday processing of life, it appears as if things that happen in my world cause my experience. My experience, then, is an effect of what happens in my world.

Imagine instead that what is occurring "out there" and my internal experience of it, are exactly like the coin mentioned earlier. The meanings or interpretations of "that" already exist in my mind. Therefore, I do not *determine* but rather *witness* what is in essence a two-sided coin—something that occurs in the world and the simultaneous meaning in my mind that I have *already* attached to it. What occurs, and my experience of it, are not separate—they are simultaneous, they are one.

We all have set beliefs, whether conscious or unconscious to us, about everything that happens in our world. We think we "know" that telling a lie is immoral, running a red light is illegal, stealing is criminal, etc. Could there be any exceptions to these? There are always other possibilities for interpretation. A woman lies to an intruder about being alone in the house to protect a child that is hiding. A man runs a red light because his wife is having a baby in the back seat. In Victor Hugo's *Les Misérables*, Jean Valjean stole bread to feed his sister's starving children.

My mind contains an entire "field of belief" I hold to be true, and this field is triggered by any one event or occurrence "out there" that intersects it. When this event or occurrence happens, the coin shows up—with two sides I may not yet recognize as being in simultaneous relationship. My experience is a reflection, not an effect. I see what I *think*, what I *believe*. And my beliefs have a purpose.

How does purpose figure into the simultaneity of *Cause and Effect*, the fixed relationship between event and reaction in my mind? Why do I react as I do? Usually, that is, unthinkingly, we experience life in a linear, "billiard ball" way, because we *want* what happens "out there" and our experience of it to be independent of one another. This does not happen by accident. It is essential I believe this because such a separation makes way for the insidious scam of victimization. I am obviously not conscious I am doing this. On the other hand, I am very conscious of how much I feel like a victim of life. Perhaps if I knew how to do it any other way, I would, but I do not, and besides, this works for me! It brings me everything I ever thought I wanted. This is a fundamental aspect of the human condition. Things happen *to* us, and we are not in control.

Victimization is the cornerstone of the foundation of human experience: "I am at the effect of the world." In the Reindeer mind, I believe the cause of my suffering is what is going on "out there." Even though *Cause and Effect* are indivisible in *Truth*, in the Reindeer mind, I not only separate them out, I reverse them. I can justify my words and actions by declaring: "I did this because you...."

Why would we want to separate what is happening "out there" from our internal experience of it? When this question is an honest one, the answer is easy: doing so allows us to believe we can escape responsibility for our experience. It is a position of blamelessness, no fault, and "false" innocence. Who among us does not live as if what is done "out there" does not affect us, does not *cause* us to think certain things, does not *cause* us to feel what we feel? This is true for the entire gamut of our personal experience, from our reaction to someone looking at us in a certain way, to our watching the various horrors and devastation that take place on our planet. Who does not think "that look" or these horrors do not *cause* them to feel what they feel? In a "billiard ball" world, I can believe what I feel is *because* of what is happening "out there."

This is the Reindeer mind's operating system, and its plan for how I can manage and cope with my experience. The whole scam is set up on the principle that "I am not the cause." I am not doing this, I am simply responding to something "other than me." I become dedicated to this line of thinking because it makes me "causeless," and only an "effect." However, once you choose to live in the Reindeer mind and occupy that universe, you are managing and coping through a faulty system, an illusion of order and meaning, and an illusion of innocence—and you are in a world of trouble. For unseen in that line of thinking is your unequivocal powerlessness. You become a helpless victim of the world. You are now and will always remain at the mercy of everything that occurs "out there."

In contrast, what does the *Truth* of the simultaneity of *Cause and Effect* offer me? If people, events, things "out there" do not *cause* my internal experience, then I am in charge. I decide, I choose, I take responsibility for my internal experience. And if I am in charge, and I do not like what I am experiencing, I can change it. Rest assured that we are not implying that such conscious responsibility is an easy thing to do. But the freedom... ah... the freedom...

The only real choice is choosing which universe you will live from, Bear or Reindeer. Once that choice is made, there are no other choices. You will experience your life as determined by that choice. In the Reindeer mind, you will believe the cause of your suffering is what is going on "out there." In the Bear mind, you recognize that suffering is a result of having chosen the wrong universe.

18

Source of Judgment

"The mark of your ignorance is the depth of your belief in injustice and tragedy. What the caterpillar calls the end of the world, the master calls a butterfly." Richard Bach

What is Judgment? It is the end result of **Changing Minds** *from* Bear *to* Reindeer. Judgment would appear to be a single act. This is not true. Instead, judgment is the culmination of a process involving several decisions: something occurs that irritates me, I *Change Minds*, I disown having done so, and I attempt to cover this up by projecting it outward onto someone or something else.

Changing Minds from Bear to Reindeer is always accompanied by guilt. And the source of that guilt is my recognition at some level (frequently unconscious) that I have *Changed Minds*, that I have denied *Truth*, that I have destroyed *Love*. My fear of having done so, or more honestly, the fear that

I will have to pay for having done so, inevitably compels me to project that guilt out into the world.

This means when I judge someone for something she has said or done, I am really only accessing my judgment of myself. What I am thinking and feeling has absolutely nothing to do with what the person I am judging said or did. Judgment is actually an exposure of my unconsciousness, my judgment of myself for having "left" *Love*. In everyday terms, I have broken my genuine connection with the other person.

The tendency is to hide my self-judgment in what is occurring, making that the justification for my response. If I believe someone is attacking me, then I respond to attack—whether or not the specifics of that attack are true. If I had not *Changed Minds*, I would not be compelled to judge at all, and regardless of what the attacker had or had not done, I could be with her very differently. I would be free to respond in an appropriate and loving (from the Bear's perspective) way.

Let's look more closely at the process of **Changing Minds** (from Bear to Reindeer), disowning and projecting that choice, which culminates in judgment. Working backwards, the motivation behind my projection is my attempt to cover up my faulty choice. The only way to do this is to make someone or something else responsible. I can then make *that* the source of my distress and no longer be responsible for my experience. In doing so, I seem to achieve an "innocence"—which is, of course, false. Moreover, it does not work, because at some level I still feel guilty. Ironically, it makes things worse, and compounds the error, because I am now guilty of both my initial mistaken choice, *and* for having unjustly attacked someone else for it.

It is no accident that the world we live in perfectly fulfills this purpose, offering us unlimited opportunities to practice this mental sleight of hand. We see even young children point the finger and proclaim, "It's not my fault. He did it!" or "She made me." And this is what we teach by our actions. But at a deeper level, I cannot overcome my fear of somehow, someday having to *pay* for my choice, with the result that all of this is driven deeper and deeper into unconsciousness, further reinforcing the cycle of projection, judgment, victimization.

Taking this further, we would affirm as a fundamental *Truth* that there are only two states of mind: my identification with *Love*, or my coping with having left—or dis-identified with—*Love*. Let us explain.

It is my identification with *Love* that allows me to *be* with whatever is occurring in my world. To "be with it" does not imply to condone it, as if you agreed with or supported it. Nor does it preclude action or an appropriate response. You could deal with someone coming at you with a knife without having to leave *Love* or judging her for attacking you. The second state of mind referred to above comes into being when you do leave *Love* and judge the "other." Then your mind is solely engaged in your absolute need to justify why you are *not* being loving.

Our objective here is to raise awareness to the level where you recognize that when you experience *judgment* toward another, such *judgment* is never about someone else or what she is saying or doing. The *judgment* is about your having C*hanged Minds* from Bear to Reindeer. You can learn that although you may not be able to change the things that occur in your world, you can remember that you are not a victim, and you can learn how to develop the habit of **Changing Minds** back from Reindeer to Bear.

What we have covered so far is how judgment operates when directed outward, which is projection. Another form of judgment occurs when judgment is directed inward: I judge myself, and this is called introjection. The most common experience of this is captured in the notion of "beating myself up" for something I did, some choice I made. In doing so, I am acting from the Reindeer mind, viewing my self as a separate object, no different than anyone else in my world. The process that occurs is identical to the process described before. The opportunity is likewise the same: to identify with *Love* and *be* with myself for whatever I have done. The other option, just as before, is to leave *Love* and punish myself for having done so.

There is a curious opportunity available in the suspension of judgment. Judgment inevitably leads you into confusion and creates a disquieted mind. It is shut off from *Love*, because it is absolutely certain it knows what is going on. When judgment is suspended, the mind quiets, and can then open to understand or appreciate what is really going on. For instance, in the case of the person attacking you with a knife, you might find compassion and understanding regarding the intensity of her pain. This does not mean that you are oblivious to the threat, and do something as stupid as let her stab you. It does mean that re-identifying with *Love* creates a condition in which you can more deeply understand what is going on—and then, of course, take whatever action is necessary.

It may look like Judgment is a basic "fact of life." Everyone judges, and judges all of the time. We are always attacking others for what they do, making them stupid or mean or wrong. Moreover, we are always doing the same thing to ourselves. Our doing so seems like an appropriate way of navigating through this world. After all, is this not what we have all learned? Judgment appears to keep us "in the know," to keep us safe, to assign everything to its proper place.

There is a particularly helpful distinction that corrects this error in thinking: discernment. Discernment is devoid of judgment, and does not attack someone for something she does, but it does not include being foolish about it either. It does so while maintaining the ability to look from the Bear perspective and remain connected to what is *True*. Discernment recognizes what actions truly mean, which results in a more appropriate response to actions that could be harmful or unsafe.   The *Source of Judgment* must be recognized if judgment is to be *relinquished*. This allows discernment to arise. We cannot escape the fact that the source of all judgment is our own guilt—not for the things that we do or have done, but from our choice to separate from *Love*.

19

Honor but not Condone

"We do not notice how opposing forces agree. Look at the bow and lyre." Guy Davenport

One of the most potentially misunderstood aspects of this *Process* has to do with honoring something, while not condoning it. To honor means to allow, to accept, to "be with" what is occurring. This misunderstanding between "honoring but not condoning" comes from the profound confusion surrounding the important distinction between *Form and Content*, discussed earlier. Remember, *Form* is about what is occurring in our physical world. *Content* is about the *meaning* we give to what is occurring. We rarely have a vote about what happens in our world. We always have a say about what it means.

It would be insane to even imply that what is occurring in our world is insignificant. Obviously, we must deal with the real events that occur in our lives. That is *Form*, and as we have determined, *Form* is not what drives our experience. But this does *not* mean that *Form* is irrelevant. The last thing in the world we would encourage is denial, for denial is futile and can actually compound the problem. Nor are we in any way pointing towards a utopian world.

At the simplest level, think of how a more astute parent might react to a child who is misbehaving. The child's misbehavior must be attended to and corrected, but this parent would do it in a loving way. It would not be loving at all to let the child continue to misbehave, as there may be consequences of the misbehavior which often cannot be avoided or undone. For example, what if a child is being rowdy and accidentally knocks over and shatters a vase? The vase remains shattered, no matter how much the child regrets his carelessness. There are consequences that cannot be overlooked or undone.

Coming from a loving place does not mean we can change what has taken place. Even more importantly, it does not mean we condone it either. If a child or spouse or friend or client acts in an unhealthy or inappropriate way, this unequivocally needs to be addressed. The real question is only about from which mind we choose to address it, the Bear or the Reindeer mind.

"Honoring, but not condoning," is the key here. It takes us directly into the paradox of living in a very real illusion. If you stop and think about this, a very real illusion sounds absurd. How can something be both real and illusory at the same time? But the paradox begins to make some sense when viewed through the optics of *Form and Content*.

This is similar to the distinction between judgment and discernment. Judgment makes a person wrong for something he has done and may open the door for what is perceived as deserved attack or retribution. Discernment, on the other hand, is the recognition that what someone has done may be unhealthy, inappropriate, or even dangerous, but this recognition does not exist in the limited realm of right and wrong. Moreover, it does not mean inaction. Condoning something carries a sense of approval, while honoring something is merely accepting it in a nonjudgmental way. The actions following judgment would be markedly different from those following discernment.

Make no mistake about this: simply condoning certain thinking or behavior is never loving and is never the real issue. Ironically, to misunderstand the true meaning of honoring is what leads to condoning. This confusion is actually a cover-up for far more insidious undercurrents of Reindeer mischief. There are many possible motives for condoning, or appearing to condone, certain behaviors. An individual might do so because he wants to be liked, or because he is afraid of confrontation. He may even be guilty of the very same behavior and realize he has no ground to stand on.

Honoring, however, comes from an entirely different place. Our capacity to honor unhealthy or inappropriate behavior stems from the part of us that intuitively understands and remembers the limits of the human condition. In this deeper, more aware place, we recognize that the human condition carries with it a great deal of pain and suffering. The inappropriate behaviors we encounter are born of our misguided attempts to cope with and manage this pain. Said another way, honoring comes from the acknowledgment that we are all Bears in *Truth*, but it is also accompanied by the awareness that far too often, we block or forget this. It is our remembrance of that *Truth* that enables us to suspend our judgment.

In the suspension of judgment, we can reinstate relationship. At first, it will seem like we have overcome something that someone did, and this is what has led to being back in relationship with that person. And on one level, this is true. What is far more important, though, is that we will discover we are actually coming back into relationship with ourselves. The issue was never—is never—about ignoring or condoning another's actions. It is always about ourselves, and our minds.

When I judge, I am not really dealing with someone else and what he did. All I am dealing with is myself, with *my Mind*. This also takes us back to our discussion in a previous chapter about *Cause and Effect*. What someone does is not and cannot be the *cause* of my reaction. My reaction can only be caused by my interpretation of these actions. When someone upsets or attacks me with words or actions, I do have a choice. I can use the event to feel threatened or insecure, and then enroll my Reindeer mind to justify my reaction, or I can move to the Bear mind and recognize that there is another way of looking at the situation.

A less obvious aspect of what occurs when we judge, when we condemn, is that we inadvertently reinforce the very system that produced the inappropriate behavior in the first place. When we judge or condone, we make the behavior the issue, and forget entirely to look at the one perpetrating the act. We overlook what that person may be dealing with, what he wants, what he needs, and most importantly, who he believes himself to be.

In contrast, when we honor, and reinstate relationship, it naturally elicits compassion and opens the possibility of insight on our part, which is a necessary precondition for any kind of loving correction. And there can be no doubt that correction under these circumstances is loving.

We want to stress again that the Bear mind is *not* about denial or living in an ideal world. It does not mean you do not get out of the way of an oncoming bus or allow someone to continue to abuse you. It does mean you remember the *Truth* of *Who You Are*, and the *Truth* of *Who* the other person *Is*, and you choose to be in relationship with your *True Self*, and with his. This will always lead to the best response in any given situation.

20

Time as Sleight of Hand

"Life can only be understood backwards; but it must be lived forwards." Soren Kierkegaard

We are going to explore *Time* both as a way to apply concepts we have already examined, as well as a means to demonstrate the truly novel concept that *time goes backwards*. From that perspective, you will discover that *Reality* appears very different indeed.

Man has attempted to measure and keep time since about 2000 BC in Sumer and Mesopotamia. From early water clocks and sundials to the most sophisticated atomic clocks now used, the tacit assumption about time is that it proceeds in a linear, forward motion.

Time has always had three parts—past, present, and future—and has always appeared to proceed in one direction, from the past through the present to the future. Let us be clear here: on the level of our three-dimensional experience of reality, this is exactly how time does work. We wake up in the morning, time proceeds forward throughout the day, then we go to sleep at night. We are born as infants and as time proceeds forward, we age, and we die. We have a past that is filled with everything we have thought and done. We have a future which is as yet unknown to us. This, however, is not the aspect of time we now wish to explore.

It is impossible to capture certain aspects of this exploration without a deeper appreciation of what *Time* is—and is not. In the normal course of events, our lives are completely trapped in time. In fact, everything is processed through time: life spans, projects, vacations, relationships, etc. Without understanding that this is how our lives are measured, it is difficult to capture the far more important attribute of Time we seek to address: Timelessness.

Timelessness is not eternity. While we might think of eternity as a long, long, very long time, timelessness is outside of all time. We approach the experience of timelessness, for example, when we are completely absorbed in doing something we have a passion for, or when we are rapt in the novelty of new love. These would include the moments when we ask: "I've been here for hours, yet it seems like mere seconds have passed. Where did the time go?" Time seems to stop for us in those instances, but at the heart of that kind of experience, time does not exist at all. Such experiences are completely outside of time.

We can also look at *Time* in terms of *Process*. We have already determined that *Consciousness* is divided into two parts, two universes, two selves: the Bear and the Reindeer. But if our *True Identity* is Bear, why do we forget this? What is in the way of our remembering? Of course, the answer is the Reindeer!

And here is the tricky part: the Reindeer lives in time, and is bound by time.

The *Sleight of Hand* referred to in the chapter title is how the Reindeer uses *Time*. The Reindeer insists on linear time and does its very best to reinforce the necessity of such thinking at every turn. For with linear time, there is guilt for past actions or inactions, anxiety for potential actions (to be done or not done), and fear of the consequences of both. The Reindeer cleverly puts us in a stress-filled bind between past and future, between guilt and fear, so that we completely squander the timeless present: this very moment in which we always must live. Do not be deceived by the confusion of levels, that is, between the physical world where we think we live as Reindeers and the timeless world of the *Truth* of ourselves as Bears.

Let us revisit the idea of the Reindeer costume. The Reindeer costume is a place where we can pretend to hide. The Reindeer would have us believe we can be "safe" under the hood of the Reindeer suit. It tells us that no one will recognize us or call us to account for our words and our actions. We can pretend to be something we are not. Sometimes, we can even fool ourselves, eating Reindeer food and playing Reindeer games—but not for long. Such self-deception can eventually lead to depression, and ultimately, to despair. This *Sleight of Hand* is a trick the Reindeer uses to keep us from *Truth*.

Time is one of the ways the Reindeer accomplishes this. In our physical world, we look at how things come into being in a linear fashion. We note that something does not exist, then with the passage of time, something appears and evolves. Take something as simple as the construction of a house. According to the laws of linear time, first, there is a vacant lot; next, a foundation is laid; then a structure is built; and finally, a house emerges.

We are not challenging that this is how a house is built. However, outside the laws of linear time, we assert that once the house is conceived, it "exists" at some level, and the construction of the house is merely the removal of anything that denies or blocks "*w*hat already is."

To grasp this, begin by imagining the lot that has been chosen for the house. If the lot is massively overgrown with weeds and underbrush, these will have to be removed in order for the construction to begin. Interestingly, the very choice of the lot is a decision "already made," because the new owner has determined that it is *possible* to clear the lot. In that sense, the cleared lot already exists in the future occupant's imagination, but the removal of the weeds and undergrowth remains a necessary step to bring the house into being.

In like manner, the Bear already always *is*. It is a decision already made. It has always existed, and it exists now, because it is timeless. It is outside of linear process. *Time* is not about the creation of something new. It is a way of remembering what already is, and always has been.

This is how time appears to work: we all live our lives as if we must struggle to overcome obstacles in the way of bringing what we want into being. We think we want to change a certain circumstance—a job, a habit, a relationship—with which we are not satisfied. In the way we usually problem-solve to cope with time, we try to make a decision about something, and then it sometimes seem as if we cannot quite decide because there are still these "obstacles" we must confront and overcome. Nothing could be further from the truth. Just as the images reported to our brains are first upside down, the *Process* in our mind operates in reverse.

Listen deeply. When we think we are making a major decision about something in our lives, we are not really encountering "obstacles" that block the decision. Instead, we are encountering the ramifications of having *already made* the decision. This is why we subject ourselves to dealing with the ramifications of our decision in the first place. Remember the house? Removing the weeds and undergrowth is not an "obstacle" to making the decision to build the house. Dealing with the overgrown lot is merely one of the ramifications of having already decided to do so. Accordingly, you roll up your sleeves, get out your tools, and do the work necessary to clear the lot.

Likewise, regarding *Process* in our *Minds*, any obstacles, or resistance we experience are not about a decision we think we are trying to make. The seeming resistance is rather about what we now must address to make manifest that which we have already decided. Many of us intuitively know the truth of this as we pretend to struggle with a difficult decision, like going back to school, or getting married or divorced, or having children, or changing jobs. We think we are weighing the pros and cons, giving fair and equal attention to both sides of the issue at hand. But in reality, once the decision is made, we can often look back and admit we always "knew" what we were to going to do. We may have had to navigate a series of "obstructions" to arrive at that conclusion, but how many times in our lives have we, in the end, skipped right over the logical blocks in our path and arrived at a decision that we knew all along we were going to make? This is because the final decision was actually made first, and then everything that interfered with the manifestation of that choice showed up to be dealt with.

With this in mind, we invite you to take another leap with us. We are pointing to the fact that you have already made the decision to be the Bear that you are in *Truth*. What you have in fact decided to do is quit pretending to be a Reindeer, because you cannot really make a decision to be something you already *are*. All you can do is stop pretending that you can deny it. Apparent obstacles to this decision will take the shape of particular people or certain events that seem to challenge you again and again and again. Your task—and the task of us all—is to go beyond all of these seeming "obstacles" and move into the timeless *Truth* of *Who You Are*.

What we *are* cannot be changed. Recognition and acceptance of this can, however, be postponed. Our obstacles are not in the way of what is *True*; they simply mask our recognition of it. That is what changes them from being obstacles to consequences of a choice.

In summary, *Time* is not moving forward through obstacles towards something to be decided. It is going backwards through the ramifications of something *already* decided.

21

You Chose into It, You Choose out of It

"Only those who risk going too far can possibly find out how far one can go." T.S. Eliot

We have looked at the power of the Witness versus the impotence of the Observer, the two-sided coin of *Cause and Effect,* and the Reindeer tricks using *Form* and *Time.* So, with much greater awareness of how we "do" our lives, what are we missing? What's the secret that unlocks the door to a different experience?

It is a simple truth that you cannot give away something that is not yours. I cannot give away your watch or your car or your house because they do not belong to me. I can give away *my* watch or *my* car or *my* house because I own them. Ownership has privilege. I am free to do whatever I please with what I own—enjoy it, enhance it, share it, or even give it away—*because* it is mine. No one operating at the level of our physical selves is going to contradict such a statement. But what happens when we apply such a concept to the *Mind?* The answer is far less obvious.

The idea of ownership is a well-kept "secret"—even, perhaps especially, from ourselves—in this *Process* of *Mind*. In the context of the thinking we have introduced, ownership is really about *responsibility*. When I am centered and aligned with what is *True*, I automatically assume responsibility for that which is mine, namely, my experience. I am aware that I give all the meaning to that which occurs to create my experience. But when I go unconscious about how experience truly happens, I am much less inclined to be responsible for what I am thinking and feeling. And I am far less able or willing to take ownership of it.

The "secret" referred to above is that each of us is always *choosing* his experience. However, most people live as if experience is just "happening" to them, as if what they are experiencing is not "chosen" by them at all. It seems as if they are just innocently going about their business, and out of nowhere, experience happens—happens to them.

This is true even at the abstract level of thought. For instance, in an anxiety attack, it appears that I am being attacked by my thoughts. The last thing I am (or want to be) aware of is that I am choosing those thoughts. But think about it: how would it be possible for someone else to choose those attack thoughts for me? Who would do the choosing, if it were not I? This is where conscious ownership comes into play, and changes everything. Hence the title of this chapter; I keep forgetting that I *Chose into It*, chose into exactly what I am experiencing.

To reiterate, the problem here is *ownership*. If I am *not* choosing the experience I am having, I cannot choose to have a different one. If I do not take ownership of my experience, I cannot "give it away," that is, change it. If I desire to have an experience other than the one I am having, I must find a part of me willing to take responsibility for having chosen my experience in the first place. Only after acknowledging that I *Chose into It*, can I ever *Choose Out of It*. I do not have to like what I have chosen to experience, but there is no way around the fact that in order to be able to *choose out* of it, I must take responsibility for it. This is what "breaks the spell" and gives me the freedom to choose something else.

More plainly, "breaking the spell" is my overcoming the denial that I—and I alone—chose it. Think about it for a minute. In any experience of your life, across the entire spectrum of utter despair to absolute joy, who but you could ever choose your experience of any specific event? Who but you could assign (and believe) the meanings that are associated with every thought, every word, every gesture, every action, and every reaction you are having?

Can you begin to see where this is heading? It is not about shame or guilt, good or bad, right or wrong. For each one of us, it is the genuine freedom offered by the increasing awareness that I alone am responsible for having chosen my complete experience.

How does this work? Taking responsibility for my experience brings me back into my *Mind*, where real change can take place. I cannot change what someone else is doing, but I can come to realize and own that my experience is never driven by something outside of me. This inevitably leads me away from believing that I am a victim of what is taking place in my world. Even further, it leads me away from the crippling idea that I am a victim of my own thoughts.

Part of what makes this so elusive is that we are talking about *Consciousness* and responsibility in a very particular way. We are not saying that as we have various experiences in life, we are consciously choosing to have those experiences. My personal experience will not be that I am actively choosing to feel alone or anxious or miserable. My experience will be that I simply feel that way. What we are saying, though, is that we cannot leave it there. This is not enough; this will not help me change how I feel.

We are talking about a different level of *Consciousness* and responsibility. We are saying that as we better understand the nature of experience, and the evolution of awareness in the *Mind*, we must (and will want to) challenge the belief that we are victims of our worlds or of our own minds. We must begin to appreciate that the key to changing our experience is first *understanding* our experience—its genesis and evolution. This means expanding our thinking to encompass the notion that if we are having a certain experience, at some level, we *chose* it. If we can get that we chose it, we can likewise get that we can choose something else. Only when we become aware of and accept responsibility for having chosen in can we ever *choose out*.

22

Awakening: What It Is

"One day Alice came to a fork in the road and saw a Cheshire cat in a tree. 'Which road do I take?' she asked. 'Where do you want to go?' was his response. 'I don't know,' Alice answered. 'Then,' said the cat, 'it doesn't matter.'" Lewis Carroll

If you do not know where you want to go, it will be very hard for you to get there. And as Lewis Carroll went on to say, "any road will take you there." But just any road will not take us to the ultimate destination of *Consciousness*. "Knowing where you are going" inherently means understanding the *Process* of *Awakening* along the way. Three different ideas, which we will explore in this and the following chapter, will help clarify this for you.

The first idea has to do with the dynamics of the *Awakening Process*. We have already explored the idea that our experience of the human condition is akin to living in a dream state. To reiterate, we have two primary states of being: awake and dreaming. Our days are spent awake, and our nights are spent dreaming. Another way to look at this would be to say that during the day we are conscious, and at night we are unconscious. Our dreaming does not mean our mind is not active; it just means our mind is engaged in another form of reality, a dream state reality, one that is structured and governed by different laws.

With respect to the two states of awake or dreaming, we find ourselves in one of the states, and then we cross some line in consciousness and enter the other one. I am awake, then I fall asleep. I am asleep, then I wake up. The *Process* of *Awakening* does not occur in the same way. We do not just "wake up" like we do as night turns to day. There is no line to cross and no change from one well-defined state to another. *Awakening* is more a *Process* of evolution. Each of us evolves, usually at a painfully slow pace, as we raise our *Awareness* of *Truth*.

The evolution of spiritual *Consciousness* follows developmental stages much in the same way ego consciousness evolves. It is essential that we begin to see, acknowledge, and honor that there are stages of development in its evolution. We do not expect a four-year-old to comprehend death, or an eleven-year-old to understand global financial markets. We would not expect a 14-year-old to grasp the subtleties of adult relationship. It would be nothing short of cruel not to recognize and honor this; otherwise, we would be holding ourselves and others to inappropriate standards that are not even meaningful as yet.

This evolution of *Consciousness* is not—and cannot be—the same for everyone. It is constrained by the boundaries of the thought system within which each of us lives, that is, the limits of our personal vocabularies, ideas, concepts, desires, history, communication, relationships, interdependence, and personal development—to name only a few. This *Process* of evolution includes our recognition that something is real—until it is not.

Things can only be understood at the level that they can be understood. There must be times in your life when you have said "That is impossible," or you have thought: "I do not believe that is true" (or "...how it happens"), and then, over time, your reality changes. You discover that something *is* possible, that it *is* true. But this usually takes place over time. It does not just happen. Developmental understanding must be acknowledged to be accepted and appreciated for what it is: developmental.

In the same vein, you cannot change something until you can. You have to look to see what is true. You do not automatically see something just because it is there. You must be willing to be wrong, to be vulnerable, to challenge your reality and to expose your erroneous thinking (which is nothing more than how you were seeing it before). Otherwise, you may not "see" it at all. It is like the hidden pictures that emerge in holographic images. They are not always immediately apparent, but under the right conditions, the images become visible, and all of a sudden, you "see" them. Of course, they were always there.

Another contributing factor is the psychological phenomenon called "perceptual blindness," a concept which some say came out of an experience described in the diaries of botanist Joseph Banks near the end of the eighteenth century. Banks accompanied Captain Cook on the *HMS Endeavor* on a scientific expedition to the south Pacific. When they arrived off the coast of Australia in April 1770, the mariners were very surprised that the presence of the ship provoked no reaction whatsoever among the natives. In other locales, there had always been a response from the natives, usually a hostile one.

The Australian historian Robert Hughes suggested that in this case, the ship "was the largest artefact [sic] ever seen on the East Coast of Australia, an object so huge, complex and unfamiliar as to defy the natives' understanding." The theory was that without a mental reference point against which to juxtapose this novel sight, the natives did not "see" the ship at all. Only when the Europeans began to come to shore in canoes did the natives react, because they understood all too well what the arrival of men in small boats meant: invasion.

Whether or not the interpretation of this historical anecdote is true, it is a terrific metaphor. For *Truth* is available to us at all times, but we have limited "sight" of it because of our overwhelming unfamiliarity with it. We often do not recognize *Truth* at all, for we have no way to process the enormity of the possibility it offers within the confines of our current thinking. Moreover, we have certain barriers and safety mechanisms in place to protect us from that which we are not yet ready to take on. When we become ready—or simply willing to be ready (and this can sometimes take place at an unconscious level)—more of *Truth* gets through to us, and we "see" differently. We understand in a way that was previously impossible.

The real point is that our advancement through the developmental stages of spiritual *Consciousness* is only possible if it is grounded in honoring exactly where we are. This requires grace on our part and it cannot be circumvented. Grace is the acceptance of things exactly as they are, without judgment. Grace, too, is developmental. Judgment shuts down *Consciousness* because it rests on the belief that we already know what is true; therefore, we have no openness to anything else. *Consciousness* responds to invitation. It requires openness, willingness, and acceptance to move away from what we think we know.

Our expectations have much the same effect on us as judgment. When we think we know where things are going, there is no opening that would allow us to be led beyond what we already know. This leaves us imprisoned in whatever level of *Consciousness* we have achieved at that point. When we do not acknowledge the developmental nature of *Consciousness*, we inevitably experience disappointment, no matter how things turn out.

Arrogance and expectation are truly the Reindeer's ultimate tools of deception. Both create limits that cannot be (or are not easily) breached. Without the awareness and acceptance of the evolution of *Consciousness* as developmental, there will always be judgment. We will always be caught within the limits of our "lesser" *Consciousness*, without the ability to merely accept those limits, not as who we truly are, but rather as who we are in this moment—with those limits.

This says nothing about our dedication, our willingness, our desire to move further. But it does leave us just as lost, drowning in a sea of erroneous shame and disappointment. We can never measure up to false or inappropriate standards, judged beyond what we have been able to obtain. All this rests on the belief that things *should* be different, that we *should* be different, that we *should* be further along than we are.

The most astounding thing of all is that such thinking completely blocks out the awareness that our acceptance of *Who We Are*, and where we are, comes from a higher level of *Consciousness*. We are not talking about or advocating excuses or resignation, but rather *Awareness*. *Awareness* fosters both acceptance and the possible need for change, honoring where we are while simultaneously inspiring us to evolve.

23

Awakening: How It Works

"We can easily forgive a child who is afraid of the dark; the real tragedy in life is when men are afraid of the light." Plato

The second idea about *Awakening* is captured in what we have found to be a particularly helpful metaphor, that of anesthesia. When you go to the hospital for a medical procedure for which a general anesthesia has been administered, your entire body goes to "sleep." As the anesthesia wears off, the body begins to wake up. But it does not do so all at once. You may find you begin to regain feeling first in your right hand, then your left foot, then your neck, etc. It is only over a period of time that you regain feeling throughout your entire body—and this process is different for everyone.

It is the same with the process of *Awakening*. We do not simply wake up and remember the *Truth* of *Who We Are*. We regain that critical consciousness of the *Truth* over time, and in varying degrees. Or consider that we are like the amnesia victim who gradually "remembers" who he is over time. But even before the memory is completely restored, nothing changes in truth. He never stops being who he is, although he does not remember it.

The third idea about *Awakening* explains how this *Process* occurs en route. Think about how a prism works. A beam of composite white light is shone into a prism, and the prism breaks the light into a rainbow of colors, a phenomenon known as refraction. Imagine such a light directed into a prism located somewhere behind us, and of which we are completely unaware. Further, imagine the prism then disperses the light into colors that are projected onto a wall in front of us. We know nothing of the prism behind us, so all we see are the colors before us. If we fixate on the colors, thinking *they* are the totality of what is real, we will never see or search for the source of the colors, the prism and the light: the *Truth*.

We have to want to see the complete picture of what is going on, and how the pieces interrelate. Until we do, even with the purest intent, we are just dealing with colors. As we move further back towards the prism, we recognize it is our mind that is generating our experience—and that changes everything.

We are much like the slaves in Plato's "Allegory of the Cave." Plato imagined a group of slaves imprisoned in a cave since childhood and chained such that their gaze was fixed forward. Behind the slaves was a fire, and between them and the fire was a raised walkway. Behind and below the raised walkway, men carrying figures of people, animals, and other objects crossed the room. The men themselves were below the walkway and cast no shadows, but the objects they carried were higher and did. The fire then cast those shadows onto the wall in front of the imprisoned slaves, who were unable to turn around and ever see or know the source of the shadows. They interpreted the shadows they saw as "reality"—and these shadows were the only reality they knew. The slaves became so accustomed to their condition that they even named the various shadows and honored the one among them who could remember the order of the shadows, and predict which shadow would come next.

Plato then supposes that one of the prisoners is freed, and is, at last, able to turn around and see the walkway and the fire. But this slave is so accustomed to darkness that the bright light of the fire hurts his eyes, and in pain, he turns away, wanting to return to the "safety" of his previous state, that is, his ignorant belief that the shadows on the wall were real. But he cannot do this, for now, he knows better. This freed slave is then forced to leave the cave, where the brilliance of the sun further intensifies his pain and discomfort. But little by little, as his eyes adjust to the light of the sun, he can see objects—not just their shadows. Over time, he is able to see a completely different reality than the only one he knew as a slave in the cave.

Something similar happens in the process of *Awakening*. Some part of our *Consciousness* begins to realize there is more going on than just what appears in front of us. As we gradually break the trance of being mesmerized by the "colors" (the false reality we see) before us, and dare to turn around and look, we are able to recognize the prism that generates the colors. As we evolve, that is, as we become more aware of *Truth*, we are further able to identify the pure white light that is being directed into the prism. We finally "see" the source of the colors.

In the human condition, we are almost hypnotized into thinking that what we see in the world is what is true. As *Consciousness* evolves, we are able to turn around and see the prism, the metaphor representing an entire thought system that produces what we think we see in the world. And note this: just because a thought system is false, does not mean it is weak. Eventually, as *Awareness* increases, we are able to look behind the prism, behind the thought system, and identify what preceded the multi-colored manifestation, that is, all we see going on around us in the world, which captivates us so. We are able to identify the composite source: *Truth.*

So where to from here?

24

Where to from Here?

"It's exhilarating to be alive in a time of awakening consciousness; it can also be confusing, disorienting, and painful." Adrienne Rich

We have spoken a lot about *Truth*. But after having recognized what we now believe is false, how can we be certain what *Truth* is? No one can define *Truth* for you, although we are doing our best to point you in the right direction to discover *Truth* for yourself. In stillness, *Truth* can be experienced. *Truth* is always *Truth*, whether or not you acknowledge it, respond to it, accept it, or practice it. Your unwillingness or inability to be with *Truth* is merely that, nothing more, and can have no effect whatsoever on *Truth* itself.

Understanding is like light, enabling us to see what would have otherwise remained unseen in the darkness of our unconsciousness. Our objective is to enable such understanding, to help you raise your *Awareness* such that *Truth* becomes evident, and like the freed slave from Plato's Cave, you willingly leave behind the closed world of false illusions that have duped you into believing that shadows are what is real. The problem with the light of *Truth* shining away the darkness is that as long as we live and believe in darkness, we instinctively want to put the light out because it exposes too much. And that fills us with fear.

The Reindeer and the Bear are both trying to convince us who we are—but the goal for the Reindeer is this world and all the trappings it seems to offer. The Reindeer can teach us how to get things in this world, but we should know—either from general observation or from direct personal experience—that money, fame, beauty, power, and things, do not bring happiness. The Bear, on the other hand, teaches that the ultimate goal is peace, which has nothing at all to do with this world. Not only does the Bear teach that it is not about "getting" anything, it teaches that it is really about "giving up" everything that stands in the way of *Truth*.

The Reindeer sees us as separate from *Truth*, separate from *Love*, separate from ourselves, lacking, needy, guilty. This leads to a state of desperation that fuels all our attacking, blaming, rejecting, and getting even. We are certainly free to believe in and make Reindeer choices, but they simply are not real. In dreams we are free to do whatever we want, breathe underwater, have magical encounters, perform daring feats of courage, etc., but when we awaken, we see that none of it was true. Only through the eyes of the Bear, who sees us as *Innocent,* free, and eternal, will we learn to forgive. And that is to *Love,* and to remember what is *Real.*

We cannot deny who we are in *Truth,* but we can definitely stifle our awareness of it. As long as we identify ourselves as physical bodies in this world, we will think that our happiness is found in whatever makes us feel safe, secure, protected; and we will then do whatever it takes to make ourselves happy—even if that includes competition, manipulation, withholding, projecting, and so forth. All this insanity is driven by attempts to preserve my "me" in the dream. It makes perfect sense, then, that pain is seen as anything that threatens that "me" or makes me unhappy. This is the Reindeer's version of our everyday lives.

The Bear, on the other hand, would counsel that pain is the experience of being separate, out of relationship, having lost all connection to *Love* and to our *True Self*. And happiness is then understood as the experience of the re-establishment of those connections. From this perspective, we see that what will make us truly happy is removing *anything* that blocks that reconnection. Fundamentally, this is the undoing of "me" in the dream.

Our *Mind* is the means by which we determine our own condition, because *Mind* is the mechanism of decision. It is the power by which we separate or join, and accordingly, experience pain or joy. The Bear sees our belief in our guilt as a mistake in thinking that is simply false. It sees only our *Innocence*. The specificity or magnitude of the mistake is irrelevant—false is false.

Moment by moment, each of us lives and teaches a reality—we each demonstrate our personal belief in what is real. And in the process, we simultaneously learn and reinforce that belief in our minds. Fortunately for us all, *Truth* is true, completely independent of us. Believing in something does not make it true any more than not believing in something makes it untrue. Untrue is untrue, period. There are no degrees of untrue. Consider the arithmetic equation: $2 + 2 = x$. There is only one correct answer for x: 4. The fact that there are lots of other numbers we could substitute for x may give us the illusion "we could choose another number," but all the other numbers, with no exceptions, would be wrong.

Too often, we are like the prodigal son who left his home to seek his happiness in the world. He tried lots of other "numbers" to fulfill the happiness equation. But one day, he woke up to the fact that all the numbers he had tried to plug into that equation were wrong—and he found himself in a pigsty. One would certainly not imagine that such an outcome could possibly be by his choice, yet it *was* the inevitable outcome of the entire series of his choosing. The chooser and the choosing and the chosen become one—and the prodigal son finally says: "I'm going home."

What we now ask you to do is take an honest look at your life—and see if you sense there is something more, something you might be missing. It is not our intent to challenge any specific background, philosophy or faith. Our intent is rather to point towards the possibility of *Awakening*, through an understanding of the dynamics of the *Mind*.

This process of *Awakening* is not easy, effortless, or pain-free. It is much like trying to stand up once your foot has fallen asleep. As you attempt to walk, you will be a little wobbly at first, and you will feel some tingling and pain. But eventually, your foot does wake up and you are fully restored to what comes naturally: walking.

The *Process* of *Awakening* does have some interesting twists. If you saw the 1999 movie, *the Matrix*, you may remember the scene where the protagonist, Neo, walks into a room of children who might be "the One." He walks over to a child who is bending spoons. Asked if he wants to try, he accepts, but he cannot bend the spoon—until the child counsels him: "Do not try to bend the spoon, for that is impossible. Bend your mind around the spoon." We are suggesting you do something similar. Do not try to change the *Form* of your life, for that may not be possible. But if you will "bend your mind" around that *Form*, whatever it may be, it will certainly lead to a different experience of your life.

The ultimate paradox about this whole *Process* is that we are not really doing anything; rather, we are *undoing*. In the end, we realize we were not even choosing, we only had the illusion of doing so. For how is it possible to choose between something and nothing? How can we choose something that does not exist?

It is sort of like that old anecdote about the drunk who is looking for his lost keys under a streetlight. A policeman comes up and asks the drunk what he is doing, and the drunk answers: "looking for my keys." The policeman then asks: "Did you lose them right here?" And the drunk replies: "No, I lost them over there, but the light is much better here."

We are suggesting that you stop looking for the "key" that will never be found in the illusory light of this world. It simply is not here. But we are pointing to where it is. We are inviting you to *Change Minds*!

This page intentionally left blank.

Glossary of Terms

The following definitions are provided to help the reader better understand how we are using each of these terms in this book. They are arranged alphabetically and may include forward references to other terms in this Glossary.

Awakening: This is what we call the *Process* of waking up to *Truth/Reality*. It includes an increasing *Consciousness* and is used in contrast to the usual state of our daily lives: unconsciousness, sleeping. The most accurate way of capturing this would to be to say that being fully *Awakened* would be synonymous with the state of *Enlightenment* (fully Bear, Reindeer-less).

awareness: When lowercase, awareness is what we operate with, are conscious of, as we live our daily lives and move thorough this world.

Awareness: When uppercase, *Awareness* is a higher, more transcendent *Consciousness*. It is what we tap into when we enter the Bear mind.

Bear, Bear universe, Bear mind: The name we have given the Self is the Bear. The Bear's universe is aligned with *Truth/Reality*, and all its experiences are processed through what we call the Bear mind. In this mind, love, forgiveness, and compassion are the guiding principles.

Center: When uppercase, *Center* is a reference point for the still and quiet place found at the core of our being. It exists outside of the Reindeer mind and world. When you are in *Center,* you experience clarity, wholeness, and harmony. The body, mind, and spirit are in balance, creating a sense of profound well-being.

Changing Minds: This is the title of the trilogy and the heart of our theory. It is italicized and bolded throughout the three books. We differentiate between ***Changing Minds***, and "changing minds about" something. The act of "changing minds about" is an attempt to merely see something differently, but this takes place in the Reindeer mind, in the Reindeer universe. In contrast, when we *Change Minds*, we leave one universe altogether, and move to the other one, from Reindeer to Bear, or vice versa.

consciousness: When lowercase, consciousness is the specific experience one is aware of as he/she makes up the meanings which constitute his/her life.

Consciousness: When uppercase, *Consciousness* refers to the context of the entire *Journey of Awakening*. It is *Awareness* that is beyond the confines of both Bear and Reindeer but includes both.

Content: *Content* contains all the meaning we give to what takes place in our lives. It is not what happens in *Form*, but what we make of it.

ego: The ego refers to the "self" that is living in this world. The ego represents anything that reinforces any belief that supports this. The ego is synonymous with the Reindeer self.

Form: *Form* accounts for anything and everything that happens in the world of space and time. *Form* carries no inherent meaning. We can never say anything about *Form* other than "this" or "that" happened.

Home: *Home* is a symbol for the place in the *Mind* that, in *Truth*, you have never left. When you are *Home*, you experience complete peace.

innocence: When lowercase, innocence is what we think we obtain in the Reindeer universe when we attempt to manage our guilt and suffering through Reindeer means. The primary mechanism we use to accomplish this is projecting that guilt and suffering outside of ourselves, believing that their cause is found in the world and in what happens to us.

Innocence: When uppercase, *Innocence* reflects the reality of the *True* nature of our being. It is the recognition that all our guilt and suffering is not only self-imposed, it is, illusory. Moreover, they have nothing to do with *Innocence*. *Innocence* is not about what we do, but about *Who We Are in Truth*. *True Innocence* cannot be lost.

Journey/Journey of Awakening: This is the *Process of* Awakening to *Truth/Reality*. It occurs through the undoing of the "self," through challenging the false Reindeer universe in the *Mind*, and through identifying more and more with *Truth* in the Bear universe.

love: When lowercase, love is affection for or attachment or devotion to someone or something. This kind of love is the way in which we interact with the world. It manifests as kindness, patience, generosity, forgiveness, etc.

Love: When uppercase, *Love* is our *True Nature,* the essence of *Who We Are in Truth.* It accounts for our connectedness to and our relationship with all things. *Love* is the universal quality of unity, unconditional acceptance, and pure beingness. *Love* is present everywhere and in everything at all times. It is the source of all Bear actions in the world.

mind: When lowercase, we refer to the mind of either the Bear or Reindeer. There is a Bear mind and a Reindeer mind, each of which contains a distinct thought system from which we operate. They are both contained in the *Mind.*

Mind: When uppercase, the *Mind* contains everything, all thoughts, all beliefs, all experiences in the past, present, and future. *Mind* contains *both* the Bear and Reindeer minds.

Parallel Universe(s): A universe is actually a philosophy, a thought system, that defines reality from a specific point of view. Our theory posits that there are two universes, two thought systems, in the *Mind,* and that these are diametrically opposed to each other. One (the Bear) is a thought system aligned with *Truth/Reality,* the other (Reindeer) with truth/reality.

process: When lowercase, process is the personal, ongoing experience of the "self," which takes place in the mind of the Bear or Reindeer.

Process: When uppercase, *Process* reflects the ongoing experience of the evolution of the *Self,* which takes place in the *Mind.*

Reindeer, Reindeer universe, Reindeer mind: The name we have given to the "self" is the Reindeer. The Reindeer resides in a universe aligned with truth/reality, (note the lowercase) and its experience is processed through what we call the Reindeer mind. In this mind, the "self" and everything associated with the "self's" personal needs are the guiding principles.

"self": When lowercase, the "self" is who we believe ourselves to be as human beings: a physical, psychological, spiritual entity living in this world.

Self: When uppercase, this concept represents a Higher Self, a Transcendent Self, a Self that is much grander than the one defined by the limits of the "self." In this trilogy, Self is synonymous with the Bear.

Spirit: *Spirit* is synonymous with the Bear self. *Spirit* represents anything that is transcendent, anything that is outside the human condition, anything that points beyond the world of the ego.

truth/reality: When lowercase, these concepts capture the essence of what it means to be a human being living in this world. It includes everything that constitutes being a physical, psychological, spiritual "self." It also includes all our ideas about the space and time world in which that "self" exists.

Truth/Reality: When uppercase, these terms convey concepts that are more transcendent. Throughout history, these terms have been used to capture the idea that there is something beyond the confines of our mere humanity, something that is absolute.

Quotes and Author Information

Opening Quote:

"Be patient toward all that is unsolved in your heart and try to love the questions themselves, like locked rooms and like books that are now written in a foreign tongue. Do not now seek the answers, which cannot be given you because you would not be able to live them. And the point is, to live everything. Live the questions now. Perhaps you will then gradually, without noticing it, live along some distant day into the answer." Rainer Maria Rilke (1875-1926), Austrian lyric poet and novelist

Chapter 1 - The Title: Changing Minds

"There is no passion to be found in playing small—in settling for a life that is less than the one you are capable of living." Nelson Mandela (1918-2013), President of South Africa 1994-1999, anti-apartheid revolutionary and philanthropist

Chapter 2 - The Subtitle: The Paradoxical Journey

"How wonderful that we have met with a paradox. Now we have some hope of making progress." Niels Bohr (1885-1962), Danish physicist and philosopher

Chapter 3 - Recognition

"Nature uses only the longest threads to weave her patterns, so that each small piece of her fabric reveals the organization of the entire tapestry." Richard P. Feynman (1918-1988), American theoretical physicist

Chapter 4 - The Bear and the Reindeer

"In short, not only are things not what they seem, they are not even what they are called!" Francisco de Quevedo (1580-1645), Spanish nobleman, writer, and politician

Chapter 5 - The Reindeer with a Halo

"We are so used to disguising ourselves to others that we end by disguising ourselves from ourselves." François VI, Duc de la Rochefoucauld, Prince de Marcillac (1613-1680), a noted French author of maxims and memoirs

Chapter 6 - Parallel Universes

"The range of what we think and do is limited by what we fail to notice. And because we fail to notice that we fail to notice, there is little we can do to change; until we notice how failing to notice shapes our thoughts and deeds." R. D. Laing (1927-1989), Scottish psychiatrist

Chapter 7 - Characteristics of the Parallel Universes

"Your problem is how you are going to spend this one odd and precious life you have been issued. Whether you're going to spend it trying to look good and creating the illusion that you have power over people and circumstances, or whether you are going to taste it, enjoy it and find out the truth about who you are." Anne Lamott (born April 10, 1954), American novelist and non-fiction writer

Chapter 8 - The Impeccability of Each Universe

"The Greek word for truth 'aletheia' doesn't mean the opposite of falsehood. It means the opposite of 'lethe,' oblivion. Truth is what is remembered." Marilyn French (1929-2009), American author

Chapter 9 - Dreaming and the Dreamer

"Without change, something sleeps inside us, and seldom awakens. The sleeper must awaken." Frank Herbert (1920-1986), American science fiction writer

Chapter 10 - Not One Self, but Two

"To the possession of the self the way is inward." Plotinus (c. 204/5- 270), Greek philosopher

Chapter 11 - The Witness and the Observer

"The greatest obstacle to discovery is not ignorance - it is the illusion of knowledge." Daniel J. Boorstin (1914-2004), American writer and historian

Chapter 12 - Waking from the Dream

"Your vision will become clear only when you look into your heart. Who looks outside, dreams. Who looks inside, awakens." Carl Gustav Jung (1875-1961), Swiss psychiatrist and psychotherapist, founder of analytical psychology

Chapter 13 - Form and Content

"The lunar flights give you a correct perception of our existence. You look back at Earth from the moon, and you can put your thumb up to the window and hide the Earth behind your thumb. Everything you've ever known is behind your thumb, and that blue-and-white ball is orbiting a rather normal star, tucked away on the outer edge of a galaxy." James Arthur "Jim" Lovell (born March 25, 1928), American former NASA astronaut

Chapter 14 - Form and Content: Purpose

"Men are disturbed not by things, but by the view which they take of them." Epictetus (c. 55-135 AD), Greek teacher and philosopher

Chapter 15 - Form and Content: Practice

"I think the greatest illusion we have is that denial protects us. It's actually the biggest distortion and lie. In fact, staying asleep in what's killing us." Eve Ensler (born May 25, 1953), American playwright, performer and feminist

Chapter 16 - Not "It" but not "Not It"

"What can we gain by sailing to the moon if we are not able to cross the abyss that separates us from ourselves? This is the most important of all voyages of discovery, and without it, all the rest are not only useless, but disastrous." Thomas Merton (1915-1968), American Catholic writer and mystic

Chapter 17 - Cause and Effect

"Because our entire universe is made up of consciousness, we never really experience the universe directly we just experience our consciousness of the universe, our perception of it, so right, our only universe is perception." Alan Moore (born 18 November 1953), English writer primarily known for his work in comic books

Chapter 18 - Source of Judgment

"The mark of your ignorance is the depth of your belief in injustice and tragedy. What the caterpillar calls the end of the world, the master calls a butterfly." Richard Bach (born June 23, 1937), American writer

Chapter 19 - Honor but not Condone
"We do not notice how opposing forces agree. Look at the bow and lyre." Guy Davenport (1927-2005), American writer, translator, painter, intellectual, and teacher. Quote from his translation from the Greek: "Herakleitos and Diogenes"

Chapter 20 - Time as Sleight of Hand

"Life can only be understood backwards; but it must be lived forwards." Soren Kierkegaard (1813-1855), Danish theologian, poet, widely considered to be the first existentialist philosopher

Chapter 21 - You Chose into It, You Choose out of It

"Only those who risk going too far can possibly find out how far one can go." T.S. Eliot (1888-1965), American poet, essayist, and playwright

Chapter 22 - Awakening: What It Is

"One day Alice came to a fork in the road and saw a Cheshire cat in a tree. 'Which road do I take?' she asked. 'Where do you want to go?' was his response. 'I don't know,' Alice answered. 'Then,' said the cat, 'it doesn't matter.'" Lewis Carroll (1832-1898), English writer, mathematician, logician

Chapter 23 - Awakening: How It Works

"We can easily forgive a child who is afraid of the dark; the real tragedy in life is when men are afraid of the light." Plato (428/427 or 424/423–348/347 BC), Greek philosopher and mathematician

Chapter 24 - Where to from Here?

"It's exhilarating to be alive in a time of awakening consciousness; it can also be confusing, disorienting, and painful." Adrienne Rich (1929-2012), American poet, essayist and feminist.

Made in the USA
Coppell, TX
13 September 2020